# 50 HIKES in

# MOUNT RAINIER NATIONAL PARK

## IRA SPRING & HARVEY MANNING

THE MOUNTAINEERS

Published by
The Mountaineers
1001 SW Klickitat Way, Suite 201
Seattle, WA 98134

© 1969, 1978, 1988, 1999 by The Mountaineers

First edition 1969. Second edition 1978. Third edition 1988
Fourth edition: first printing 1999, second printing 2002, third printing 2004

Published simultaneously in Great Britain by Cordee, 3a DeMontfort Street, Leicester, England, LE1 7HD

Edited by Christine Clifton-Thornton
Maps and book layout by Marge Mueller, Gray Mouse Graphics
All photographs by Bob and Ira Spring unless otherwise noted
Cover and book design by Jennifer Shontz

Cover photograph: *14,410-foot-high Mount Rainier and Little Reflection Lake, Mount Rainier National Park.*
Title page*: Sunset near Seattle Park, Hike 17.*

*Library of Congress Cataloging-in-Publication Data*

Spring, Ira.
    50 hikes in Mount Rainier National Park / Ira Spring & Harvey Manning. — 4th ed.
        p.    cm.
        Includes index.
        ISBN 0-89886-572-7
        1. Hiking—Washington (State)—Mount Rainier National Park—Guidebooks. 2. Mount Rainier National Park (Wash.)—Guidebooks. I. Manning, Harvey. II. Title. III. Title: Fifty hikes in Mount Rainier National Park
GV199.42.W22 M687 1999
917.97'7820443—dc21

                                                                98-58157
                                                                    CIP

 Printed in Singapore by Star Standard Industries Ltd.

# CONTENTS

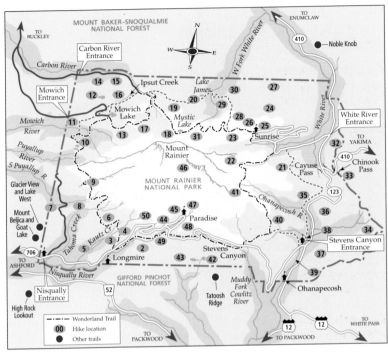

# KEY TO MAP SYMBOLS

| | |
|---|---|
| ═══ | paved road |
| ─── | improved road (coarse gravel or dirt) |
| ▪▪▪▪ | primitive (jeep) road |
| ──┼── | gated road |
| - - - - | trail |
| -··-··- | Wonderland Trail |
| ·········· | cross-country route |
| -··-··- | park boundary |
| (97) | U.S. highway |
| (530) | state route |
| [26] | county route |
| [3060] | National Forest route |
| /643/ | trail number |
| ⌂ | building |
| ⬤ | ranger station |

| | |
|---|---|
| ▲ | campground |
| ⬆ | wilderness patrol cabin |
| ◼ | shelter |
| ⌂ | wilderness campsite |
| 🏛 | lookout |
| )[ | bridge |
| )( | pass |
| ∼∼ | river or stream |
| ⋕ | waterfall |
| 🟦 | lake |
| ⚘ | marsh |
| ▬ | glacier |

5

# FOREWORD

The Webster's Dictionary offers 20 different definitions for the term "trail," but none can describe the experience one gets from rounding a bend at Mount Rainier National Park and seeing the great volcano framed by an alpine meadow awash in wildflowers. Parks are places of discovery, about the environment, about our history, about ourselves, and *50 Hikes in Mount Rainier National Park* is a great guide to those discoveries. In the deep, green forests of the Cascades, along the great shoulders of the mountain, and up to the headwaters of glacial rivers, each trail offers hikers an opportunity to experience the wonders of this great park in their own ways, on their own time. Whether novice or trail-hardened veteran, this guide can help you find the right place and the right trail to get you there and back, safely.

Whether you are strolling with family along the Trail of the Shadows or puffing with full pack up the next ridge on the Wonderland Trail, the hikes in Mount Rainier offer a window into wilderness and into a slower and simpler time. The National Park Service takes great pride in being the steward of Mount Rainier National Park for the American people, and we work hard to keep the trails in good condition for your enjoyment and access. We need your help every day to be successful in that goal, so bring one more essential along with the "Ten Essentials" that may save your life in an emergency. That one more essential is respect for the fragile environment of the mountain. That essential will help us protect Mount Rainier National Park and all its wonderful trails for generations to come.

—— *Jonathan B. Jarvis, Superintendent, Mount Rainier National Park, 2002*

▼ *Sunrise from Panhandle Gap*

# INTRODUCTION

*In their journey westward from the Great Lakes across the Great Plains and the Great American Desert, over the Big Muddy and under the Big Sky, passing sidetrails to the Grand Teton and Big Hole and Gros Ventre, and to the Great Salt Lake and the Great Central Valley, and to the Grand Canyon and Rio Grande, the pioneers gazed upon and heard about a goodly amount of sizeable geography. Nevertheless, at Puget Sound they were struck dumb, or as near to it as a pioneer could be, by the hugest lump of free-standing American earth ever in view of a prairie schooner, so almighty high that the upper reaches were winter-white the whole summer long. Had they felt the need for an outside opinion, they (or their children, anyhow) could have quoted John Muir, who after completing the eighth (or thereabouts) ascent in 1888, proclaimed that, "Of all the fire mountains which, like beacons, once blazed along the Pacific Coast, Mount Rainier is the noblest." His imprimatur helped establish "The Mountain,"in 1899, as Washington's first national park.*

> —— *Conservation and Conflict: The U.S. Forest Service and National Park Service in the North Cascades 1892–1992,* by Harvey Manning, North Cascades Conservation Council, Seattle, 1992

The National Park Act of 1916 declares that the purpose of Mount Rainier National Park is "to conserve the scenery and the natural and historic objects and the wildlife . . . ." Each visitor must therefore enjoy the park "in such manner and by such means as will leave it unimpaired for the enjoyment of future generations." A good motto for park users is: "Take only pictures. Leave nothing."

The first national parks were set aside in an era when frontier country was being recklessly exploited by "today" men equally unaware of yesterday and tomorrow. Even then, however, when empty lands seemed inexhaustible, some Americans recognized that such climaxes of scenery as Mount Rainier's were too precious to be left open to wanton desecration. Now, as in the beginning of the concept, a national park is the highest protection Americans give their land, the purest expression of a nature-sensitive ethic.

## TRAILS

Most of the trails in Mount Rainier National Park were built generations ago by people in a hurry to get somewhere, and they vary from steep to very steep. There are three types of trails:

1. *Designated trails,* which comprise the majority of the park's trails, are the only ones described in this book. These trails were designed and/or built

by the Park Service and are marked on maps and signed. Except for a few seldom-used miles, they are exceptionally well maintained.

2. *Way trails* are boot-beaten paths that may be minimally maintained to prevent excessive environmental damage but were not built or designed by the Park Service and are not marked on maps or signed.

3. *Social trails* are made by people taking shortcuts across meadows. The Park Service spends a lot of its resources rehabilitating meadows damaged by social (antisocial!) trails.

On the whole, the park has the best-built and best-maintained trails of any area in Washington, offering many miles of wide, smooth paths. Conditions are especially good in forests; in alpine meadows, where the short season makes maintenance difficult, the tread is sometimes sketchy.

As soon as the snow melts, trail crews cut away fallen trees and repair winter damage. River crossings are the worst problem. The glacial streams flood and change course and wash out bridges with exasperating frequency. Much of the flooding occurs in June, and it may be mid-July before all the bridges are replaced. If planning a hike before that date, be sure to find out at a park entrance or ranger station whether the necessary bridges are in place.

Memorial Day is the annual target date to replace bridges lost during spring floods and to put the walking boards back on the suspension bridges. In addition to the lack of bridges, early season hikers may encounter major tree blowdowns that block trails. May and June are notorious for late avalanches that often plunge far below the normal snowlines. Trails above 4000 feet may be hidden under 10 feet of snow until July, making navigation difficult in good weather and darn near impossible in a fog. Prior to July and after mid-September, hikers are advised to carry ice axes.

**Note:** As of this writing, the West Side Road shuttle bus (see Hikes 6 to 10) is not yet in place. Call the park for an update before you go.

## MAPS

The Mount Rainier contour map in the 7.5-minute series, the Trails Illustrated map, as well as the Green Trails version (available for purchase at map stores and the park's visitor centers) should be carried and consulted by any party taking a long trip. An accurate lithographed pictorial map of the park, painted by Dee Molenaar from 1960 aerial photographs, is also available. There's no substitute for a highway map; if you can't read that, you are lost in the city, so stay there and hope somebody finds you. (Call 911.)

## PETS

Mount Rainier trails are for people and for the animals who live there. Pets are not allowed on any trail in the park. Wildlife quickly disappears when a dog starts sniffing around—except, maybe, a bear who is angered by the barking and thus becomes a danger to people. The rule against pets

*Yellowstone cliffs on Windy Gap trail* ▶

covers even the smallest dog or cat, pets on leash, pets carried in arms, and pets walking to one side of the trail and thus technically "not on it." There are no boarding kennels in the park, so pets should be left at home.

Dogs bother not only wild animals but tame people as well. Most complaints come from hikers who have been harassed by noisy dogs or have found excrement in their assigned campsites. Rangers are required to give a citation whenever a dog is found in the backcountry.

Horses are allowed on a few trails in the park, but their impact on the terrain requires careful management. A party wishing to travel by horse must contact park headquarters at Ashford to check on the trails that are open to horse use before the trip.

## CLOTHING

Street shoes and city clothing are fine for nature walks and short forest trails, but any long trip—especially at high altitudes—calls for something better. (Hikers arriving at Mount Rainier without proper gear can rent boots from the guide service at Paradise.) Sturdy, lug-soled boots are essential for safety and enjoyment on slippery mud and snow, of which Rainier has its share.

Anyone hiking more than an hour from the road must give careful thought to clothing—and the weather. A clear morning is no guarantee it won't be raining by noon, and though being soaked an hour's walk from a dry car is a minor misery in the lowlands, above treeline the experience can be serious.

Mount Rainier makes its own weather, often in a hurry and without warning. Warm sunshine may give way in minutes to a cold, damp fog, and in minutes more to driving rain or snow. A person clothed only for sunshine should turn around and head for home at the first sign of changing weather. Better yet, of course, is to be prepared for the worst by carrying a pack containing a sweater and a hooded windbreaker, raincoat or poncho, and rain pants or chaps.

There is no way to stay dry while hiking in a heavy rain. The maximum hope is to shed some of the water and meanwhile keep warm. Waterproof garments hold the rain out and the perspiration in—the hiker gets wet from the inside. No matter how high the price or how extravagant the advertising claims, the "miracle" fabrics may indeed let the sweat "breathe out," but after a few hours in a downpour, they let the rain leak in. When wearing waterproof or water-repellent garments, it is wise to slow down to avoid overheating.

Some prefer to hike in shorts and T-shirts, getting sopping wet but maintaining warmth by moving at a steady pace; at camp they then put on dry clothing from the pack. If—and only if—one has the dry clothing, this is a reasonable method, especially on overnight trips. The best strategy for most circumstances is to wear wool clothing (trousers and shirt) which provides warmth even when wet. However, backpacker shops offer a variety of high-tech, high-priced alternatives to wool—garments bubbled out of a chemist's pot and painted up as pretty as butterflies.

The need for plenty of warm clothing when hiking above treeline cannot be stressed too much. There have been more fatalities in the park from exposure leading to hypothermia (subnormal body temperature) than from climbing accidents. Wind and wet weather on simple and easy trails have killed more people than icefalls. A study by the U.S. Army Surgeon General shows a wind speed of 15 miles per hour and a temperature of 67 degrees F (which should be considered fairly "balmy" conditions in Mount Rainier meadows) are as chilling as a still-air temperature of 23 degrees F. Even in midsummer, Mount Rainier hikers often encounter 35-mile-per-hour winds and 39-degree temperatures—the "chill equivalent" of a still-air minus-38 degrees F. The combination of wind and rain or snow is even more lethal.

Hypothermia is insidious in the way it creeps up unrecognized; experienced mountaineers are caught almost as often as beginners. By the time a person realizes he is not merely weary, shivering, sluggish, and awkward of body and mind, but is suffering from hypothermia, he may have no strength left to save himself. Indeed, the mind typically becomes too dulled to be aware of danger. The victim sinks to the ground to rest "for just a minute" and slips unaware into a final sleep. The lesson is obvious: A person who lacks sufficient clothing, shelter, and food should start for safety at the first hint of bad weather—going back to the car, or at least down to timberline.

## OTHER EQUIPMENT

Proper boots and clothing, plus perhaps a sandwich or candy bar stuffed in the pocket, will suffice for the shorter and easier Mount Rainier hikes. The longer and more complicated trips demand the fuller outfit discussed in *Mountaineering: The Freedom of the Hills* (The Mountaineers, 1996).

From years of experience, some of it tragic, The Mountaineers have developed a list of items that should be carried by every person on any extended walk—items that provide the minimum conditions for survival when an accident or loss of route or sudden storm makes the trip longer or more severe than expected. Every person should carry these Ten Essentials—some in the pockets, others in the rucksack.

1. Extra clothing.
2. Extra food. (The test: Is there something left over at the end of the trip?)
3. Sunglasses. (Without them even a short snow crossing can be uncomfortable; prolonged snow travel can damage the eyes.)
4. Knife. (A simple pocket variety is enough; uses include first aid and emergency fire-building.)
5. Matches. (Waterproof or in a waterproof container.)
6. Firestarter. (Chemical fuels, easy burning, for starting an emergency fire with wet wood.)
7. First aid kit.
8. Flashlight.
9. Map.
10. Compass.

## CAMPING, FIRES, AND FEES

Camping is the most damaging of all uses of fragile alpine meadows and if not carefully controlled quickly turns them into dustbowls. To preserve highland gardens the Park Service has initiated a backcountry-use permit system. Wilderness permits are required for camping at any time of the year. They may be obtained for specific campsites at any ranger station during regular business hours on a first-come, first-served basis.

In addition to permits for designated camps, off-trail ("cross-country") permits are issued to give the experienced hiker a chance for solitude. Wood fires are banned at all camps and from all off-trail camping.

Some of the designated camps have small open-ended shelter cabins. The shelters are available on a first-come, first-served basis; since they hold only three or four people comfortably, most backpackers carry a plastic tarp or a lightweight alpine tent.

In olden days (when the authors of this book were young), hikers cushioned hard wilderness beds with masses of boughs. This was just one of the bad things that were customary in the good old days of a less-crowded world but that now are anti-social and (in Mount Rainier National Park) illegal. The proper wilderness citizen buffers bones with an air mattress or a foam plastic pad.

The wood fire, beloved since days of the caves, also is obsolete. The easy wood was all burned up years ago. What remains is part of the scenery, no more deserving to be set afire than the paintings at the Louvre. A roaring blaze is as happy an event now as it was in the time of those shivering old Ice Age caves, and may still be enjoyed in forest campgrounds—if you stop by the supermarket before leaving town and load the car with a few chunks of seasoned maple.

For a hot meal, backpackers need to carry a lightweight stove for cooking. The alternate is to not cook ("Though the food is cold the inner man is hot") and to depend on clothing and shelter (and evening strolls) for warmth. The "minimalist" hiker who is beginning to replace the "tekky" finds less pleasure in fooling with a fussy stove and stewing a pot of freeze-dried than peacefully bundling up in parka/sleeping bag and supping on a sandwich and cupcake while quietly watching the sun go down and the stars come out.

## WATER

Hikers traditionally have drunk the water in wilderness in confidence, doing their utmost to avoid contaminating it so the next person also can safely drink. But there is no assurance your predecessor has been so careful. No open water ever, nowadays, can be considered safe for human consumption. Any reference in this book to "drinking water" is not a guarantee. It is entirely up to the individual to judge the situation and decide whether to take a chance.

In the late 1970s began a great epidemic of giardiasis, caused by a vicious little parasite that spends part of its life cycle swimming free in water, part in the intestinal tract of beavers and other wildlife, dogs, and people. Actually, the "epidemic" was solely in the press; *Giardia* was first identified in the eighteenth century and is present in the public water systems of many cities of the world and many towns in America—including some in the foothills of the Cascades. Long before the "outbreak" of "beaver fever" there was the well-known malady, the "Boy Scout trots." This is not to make light of the disease; though most humans feel no ill effects (but become carriers), others have serious symptoms that include devastating diarrhea, and the treatment is nearly as unpleasant. The reason giardiasis has become "epidemic" is that there are more people in the backcountry—more people drinking water contaminated by animals, more people con-

▲ *Filtering drinking water during a lunch break below Windy Gap*

taminating the water.

Whenever in doubt, keep in mind that *Giardia* can survive in water at or near freezing for weeks or months—a snow pond is not necessarily safe. Boiling for 10 minutes is 100 percent effective against not only *Giardia* but also the myriad other filthy little blighters that may upset your digestion or—as with some forms of hepatitis—destroy your liver.

Since boiling requires a fire, a better method is to use one of the several *iodine* treatments (chlorine compounds have been found untrustworthy in wildland circumstances), such as Potable Aqua or the more complicated method that employs iodine crystals.

Most backpackers use water filters, but whether they cope with invisible contaminants as effectively as the manufacturers advertise is debatable; iodine is cheaper and never fails.

### CROSS-COUNTRY HIKING

The 1964 Wilderness Act specifically states: "where the Community of Life is untrammeled by man, where man himself is a visitor who does not remain."

Much of the Park backcountry is trailless, kept that way to preserve some areas in as natural a condition as possible. Off-trail roaming in a pristine environment gives a hiker a sense of exploring, a degree of solitude, and adventure, but with it comes a responsibility for the environment, your own well-being and knowledge of safe mountain travel; leaving the trail-less area "untrammeled" must be taken seriously.

The trailless area within the boundaries of Mount Rainier National Park are relatively small and extremely fragile, and those can accommodate only a few off-trail explorers. While most plants are resilient enough to with-stand one or two footsteps, they will be crushed by footsteps repeated again and again. Even crossing a rock slide will disturb lichen and tiny plants that may have taken a century to grow.

At the Wilderness Information Centers, the Park Service has a limited number of cross-country permits to give to experienced hikers. When ob-taining the permit, the applicant will be interviewed by the ranger to make certain he or she understands the fundamentals of No Trace Hiking.

### WEBSITE

Up-to-date trail information is posted on Mount Rainier National Park's own website www.nps.gov/mora. Click on Quick Link, next Recreational Activities, then backpacking, and finally Planning a Wilderness Trip.

### LITTER AND GARBAGE

Ours is a throwaway civilization, but it is bad wildland manners to leave litter for someone else to worry about, especially in a national park. The rule among thoughtful hikers is: If you can carry it in full, you can carry it

▲ *Cross-country camping near Moraine Park*

rule among thoughtful hikers is: If you can carry it in full, you can carry it out empty.

Other actions should be self-evident matters of ecological courtesy.

On a day hike, take back to the road (and garbage can) every last orange peel and gum-wrapper. On an overnight hike, carry back everything, including metal, plastic, glass, and paper.

Don't bury garbage. If fresh, animals will dig it up and scatter the remnants. The park is not large enough to hide underground all the cans and bottles and debris. Tin cans may take more than 80 years to disappear completely; aluminum and glass last for centuries. Further, digging pits to bury junk disturbs the groundcover, and iron often leaches from buried cans and "rusts" springs and creeks.

Don't leave leftover food for the next travelers; they will have their own food and won't be tempted by contributions spoiled by time or chewed by animals.

Especially don't cache plastic tarps. Weathering quickly ruins the fabric, little creatures nibble, and the result is a useless, miserable mess.

## BEARS

If every hiker were to scrupulously avoid advertising himself as proprietor of a traveling supermarket, the "bear problem" would completely disappear in a very few years, the animals quickly reverting to their natural foods. This must become every hiker's goal.

The problem cannot be solved by merely hanging food bags from trees. Bears that develop a dependence on man's bounty quickly learn to climb the tree and make a flying leap for the bag. It is necessary for all—not just some—hikers to conspire to keep from bears the secret that backpackers carry eatables. This may be done by never leaving a scrap of garbage, not even cracker crumbs "for the chipmunks," and never tossing bacon grease or fish guts or the like in the bushes. Pack it out.

If allowed sufficient time, a hungry bear will inevitably gain access to an untended food cache. Always keep food in tight containers to prevent aromas from spreading in the breeze. Always keep these containers in a tough food bag in a closed pack near the party. Hanging food between trees is effective, but park personnel are concerned about damage done to frequently used trees. Although difficult to find in the lower 48 states, special odor-proof bags used by hikers in Alaska are recommended by the park supervisor.

## THEFT

Twenty years ago theft from a car left at a forest or national park trailhead was rare. Not now. Equipment has become so fancy and expensive, so much worth stealing, and hikers so numerous, their throngs creating large assemblages of valuables, that theft is a growing problem. Not even wilderness camps are entirely safe; a single raider hitting an unguarded camp may easily carry off several sleeping bags, a couple of tents, and assorted stoves, down booties, and freeze-dried strawberries—maybe $1000 worth of gear in one load! However, the professionals who do most of the stealing mainly concentrate on cars. Authorities are concerned but can't post guards at every trailhead.

National park rangers have the following recommendations. First and foremost, don't make crime profitable for the pros. If they break into a hundred cars and get nothing but moldy boots and tattered T-shirts, they'll give up. The best bet is to arrive in a beat-up 1960 car with doors and windows that don't close and leave in it nothing of value. If you insist on driving a nice new car, at least don't have mag wheels, tape deck, and radio, and keep it empty of gear. Don't think locks help—pros can open your car door and trunk as fast with a picklock as you can with your key. Don't imagine you can hide anything from them—they know all the hiding spots. If your hike is part of an extended car trip, arrange to store your extra equipment at a nearby motel.

Be suspicious of anyone loitering around a trailhead. One of the tricks of the trade is to sit there with a pack as if waiting for a ride, watching new arrivals unpack—and hide their valuables—and maybe even striking up a conversation to determine how long the marks will be away.

The ultimate solution, of course, is for hikers to become as poor as they were in the olden days. No criminal would consider trailheads profitable if the loot consisted solely of shabby khaki war surplus.

## THIS LAND IS YOUR LAND

Some of the preceding paragraphs may strike a hiker raised in the frontier tradition as being too heavy on "don'ts." However, neither The Mountaineers nor the National Park Service seeks to restrict freedom of enjoyment. Rather, the intent is to suggest how one may enjoy the park without destroying the pleasure for others who will follow the same trails tomorrow, next summer, and in years to come.

Mount Rainier National Park is the property of every American. For each of us and all of us, it is home, if we make it so, and treat it so.

## SAFETY CONSIDERATIONS

The reason the Ten Essentials are advised is that hiking in the backcountry entails unavoidable risk that every hiker assumes and must be aware of and respect. The fact that a trail is described in this book is not a representation that it will be safe for you. Trails vary greatly in difficulty and in the degree of conditioning and agility needed to enjoy them safely. On some hikes routes may have changed or conditions deteriorated since the descriptions were written. Also, trail conditions can change even from day to day, owing to weather and other factors. A trail that is safe on a dry day or for a highly conditioned, agile, properly equipped hiker may be completely unsafe for someone else or unsafe under adverse weather conditions.

You can minimize your risks on the trail by being knowledgeable, prepared, and alert. There is not space in this book for a general treatise on safety in the mountains, but there are a number of good books and public courses on the subject, and you should take advantage of them to increase your knowledge. Just as important, you should always be aware of your own limitations and of conditions existing when and where you are hiking. If conditions are dangerous, or if you are not prepared to deal with them safely, choose a different hike! It's better to have a wasted drive than to be the subject of a mountain rescue.

These warnings are not intended to scare you off the trails. Hundreds of thousands of people have safe and enjoyable hikes every year. However, one element of the beauty, freedom, and excitement of the wilderness is the presence of risks that do not confront us at home. When you hike you assume those risks. They can be met safely, but only if you exercise your own independent judgment and common sense.

## MORE INFORMATION

All trails in this book (except the few in the "Other Trails" section) are administered by the National Park Service. For further information write to Mount Rainier National Park, Tahoma Woods, Star Route, Ashford, Washington 98304; or call (360) 569-2211.

## EXPLANATION OF SYMBOLS

**1** **Short and easy strolls.** An hour or a loitering afternoon. Good for anyone at all, equipped with any reasonable sort of footwear, any clothing sufficient for ordinary modesty.

**2** **Moderate hikes.** A substantial portion of a day for a person in average "city" health and physical condition. Sturdy walking shoes or lightweight boots, clothing from head to toe sufficient to protect against the worst weather visible on the horizon plus extra in the rucksack as one of the Ten Essentials (see earlier in this section).

**3** **Strenuous hikes.** A lengthy day, recommended only for those in fair to excellent "mountain" condition. Considerable number of miles of trail and feet of elevation gain. Lug-soled boots, clothing to cope with low temperatures, high winds, and rain or snow. Ten Essentials, of course (see earlier in this section), and for overnighters, camping gear.

⌂ Trails with campsites available for overnight trips.

# 1 THE WONDERLAND TRAIL

**Complete loop:** 95.2 miles
**Total elevation gain:** 20,000 feet
**Hikeable:** mid-July through late September

Trail Number One it indisputably is, by rights of merely a few steps less than 100 miles of walking, and a cumulative elevation gain that, if strung vertically together, would lead from sealevel to the summit of North America; and most importantly, by introduction and pretty much hitching up into a grand and glorious unity all the other trails of Mount Rainier described in these pages: all the many and varied aspects of The Mountain.

As the devout go on pilgrimage to Mecca or Canterbury, so the "end-to-ender" walks from Mexico to Canada on the Pacific Crest Trail—and so, too, does the "round-the-mountaineer" encircle Rainier on the Wonderland Trail. There is satisfaction in the feat itself, as in running a marathon or ascending all the world's peaks of 8000 meters. However, the essence of the thing is the *wonder* of it. The name came as reflexively as a gasp to those who built the trail in 1915, and to the members of The Mountaineers who walked the circuit on their Summer Outing before construction was complete.

Any mountain is best seen not from the top but from the bottom, or somewhere near. Especially is this true of *The* Mountain. Not too far north,

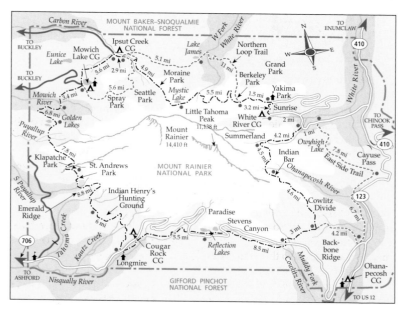

▲ *Tahoma Creek suspension bridge on the Wonderland Trail*

not too far south, fortuities of latitude and maritime climate combine with elevation to give Rainier the largest single-peak glacier system of the old 48 states and—cheek-by-jowl with the white—as gaudy a rainbow panoply as brightens any place in the world. At this precise point in North America is the optimum coincidence, side by side, of glaciers and flowers.

The wonder of the Wonderland Trail is that it passes through every life zone of the national park, from valley forests to alpine meadows to high barrens of rock and snow. Along the way are trees, flowers, animals, and glaciers. And views: So different does Rainier look from various segments, it's difficult to recognize it as all the same mountain. As the summit of Rainier is to a climber, so the Wonderland Trail is to a hiker—the experience of a lifetime.

A strong hiker can do the entire trail in a single week, but 10 to 14 days are about average and much more enjoyable. To allow for full appreciation of scenic highlights and time for sidetrips, a party should spend 2 weeks or more—not forgetting extra time for sitting out several or so days of rain. Other hikers spread the hike over 2 or 3 years, hiking just a portion of the trail for a week each year. In each case, transportation must be arranged to avoid doubling back.

Supplies for the entire trip can be carried from the beginning, but this makes for hard, slow walking in the early days. A better plan is to deposit food caches beforehand at two automobile-accessible intermediate points around the circle, or arrange to be met at those points by friends bringing the supplies. Ranger stations will store food for you but cannot store any type of fuel. Longmire, Sunrise, and Paradise Ranger Stations are regularly staffed during the summer season and open during normal business hours. However, other ranger stations, such as Mowich Lake and White River, are open only at irregular hours and some days not at all. There is no place along the route to buy staples except the concession at Longmire; meals can be purchased at Sunrise, Paradise, and Longmire for a change from backpack menus.

Be prepared for rain by carrying a tent or tarp. Few parties are lucky enough to complete the entire trip without a few days of mist, downpour, or perhaps snow—which can and does fall on the high meadows throughout the summer. The few, small shelter cabins cannot be counted on; they are frequently taken by other groups. Other details of equipment and planning are covered in the Introduction.

Camping along the Wonderland Trail is allowed only at specifically designated trailside campsites. A wilderness permit is required for each night of camping.

There are twenty-two designated trailside campsites, three campgrounds that can be reached by car (four if the Carbon River Road is open). Since campsites are not evenly spaced at 9- to 10-mile intervals (what the average hiker covers each day), a hiker who wishes to cover 13 to 14 miles must think ahead. When planning the itinerary and judging where to camp, take into consideration the elevation gains between camps as well as the distances.

In applying for a permit, list every camp you plan to use and the dates. Have alternate campsites in mind in the event your first choice is full on a given night. If unable to keep to your schedule, contact the wilderness ranger for help to change your itinerary. Because wilderness campsites are limited, hikers are urged to start in midweek, increasing the likelihood of getting their first choice camping spots.

The Wonderland Trail is described here starting at Longmire solely because that point has bus service; no need to drive your car from Chicago to do this American classic. There is no best starting point; they are all good. It makes no difference which way one hikes the Wonderland Trail, counterclockwise or, as described here, clockwise. The views are great no matter which way the eyes are pointed.

## PART I: LONGMIRE TO MOWICH LAKE

**One-way trip:** 34.3 miles
**Allow:** 4 to 7 days
**High point:** 5900 feet
**Elevation gain:** 5900 feet
**Hikeable:** mid-July through September

The Wonderland Trail begins in forest and climbs to meadows, dips into trees and rises into flowers, again and again, passing close to the Tahoma and Puyallup Glaciers, and traverses the entire west side of The Mountain. There are seven wilderness trailside camps, at 3 miles, 5 miles, 11.1 miles, 14.8 miles, 17.6 miles, 22.6 miles, and 29.4 miles. Before starting, make certain you can handle the suspension bridge at Tahoma Creek (see comments in Hike 6); there is no alternate route.

*From Longmire* it is a short 3-mile climb over Rampart Ridge to Pyramid Creek wilderness camp for an elevation gain of 1400 feet and a loss of 300 feet. *From Pyramid Creek* the next wilderness camp at Devils Dream Creek is only 2 miles farther and 1000 feet higher. *From Devils Dream* it is 6 difficult but scenic miles to South Puyallup River wilderness camp, as the Wonderland Trail climbs into the flower fields of Indian Henry's Hunting Ground (Hike 6) and drops 1700 feet to the dancing Tahoma Creek suspension bridge. From the bridge, the Wonderland Trail climbs 1400 feet over the prow of Emerald Ridge (Hike 8) and descends to South Puyallup River wilderness camp. Total elevation gain, 2100 feet, with a loss of 2900 feet.

*From South Puyallup River* the way climbs steeply to meadowland, skirts St. Andrews Lake, and still in meadows descends to Aurora Lake in Klapatche Park (Hike 9) and the most beautiful wilderness campsites on the trail, a distance of only 3.5 miles from the South Puyallup River and an elevation gain of 1900 feet and a loss of 400 feet. *From Klapatche Park* the trail goes back into forest, losing another 1900 feet in 2.8 miles to North Puyallup River wilderness camp. From the river the trail climbs again into

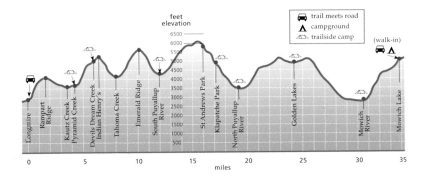

parkland to Golden Lakes Camp in Sunset Park (Hike 10), a distance of 5 miles with an elevation gain of 1200 feet and a loss of 200 feet.

*From Golden Lakes* the Wonderland Trail leaves meadowland and descends into woods to Mowich River wilderness camp, 6.8 miles from Golden Lakes, with an elevation loss of 2400 feet. *From Mowich River* the trail climbs 2300 feet in 3.4 miles to the road at Mowich Lake.

## PART 2: MOWICH LAKE TO WHITE RIVER
**One-way trip:** 26.1 miles
**Allow:** 3 to 6 days
**High point:** 6700 feet
**Elevation gain:** 5200 feet
**Hikeable:** mid-July through September

The second, and most remote, section of the Wonderland Trail rounds the cold north side of The Mountain, passing under looming Willis Wall and through flower meadows on the slopes of small peaks. There are six wilderness trailside camps along this section, at 5.6 miles, 8.5 miles, 9.6 miles, 13.4 miles, 18.9 miles, and 24 miles.

*From Mowich Lake* the trail is fairly level to Ipsut Pass and then drops steeply to Ipsut Creek Campground (Hike 16), an easy and quick 5.6 miles with plenty of time for a sidetrip to Eunice Lake and Tolmie Peak (Hike 12). However, there is a more strenuous but very rewarding alternate route, to Carbon River by way of Spray Park (Hike 13) and Seattle Park (Hike 17), traversing miles of alpine flower fields before descending to Carbon River wilderness camp with an elevation gain of 1700 feet and a loss of 3200 feet in 8 miles. The hike could be broken at either Eagle's Roost or Cataract Valley wilderness camp along the way.

*From Ipsut Creek Campground,* the Wonderland Trail goes up the Carbon River valley 3 miles (see Hike 18) and joins the alternate route at Carbon River wilderness camp. *From Carbon River wilderness camp* it crosses a

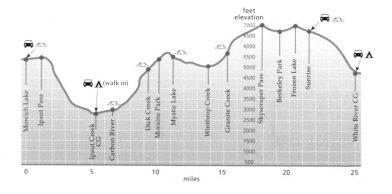

▲ *Star tracks and Mount Rainier from near Seattle Park*

bouncy suspension bridge. (If the bridge worries you, see Hike 14 for an alternate route.) Leaving the bridge the trail climbs past the snout of the Carbon Glacier to Dick Creek wilderness campsite, a long 4.2 miles (an elevation gain of 1800 feet) from Ipsut Creek. *From Dick Creek* the trail enters flower gardens with a great view of Willis Wall and descends 300 feet to Mystic wilderness camp, 3.8 miles from Dick Creek. *From Mystic* the next camp is 5.5 miles down past the snout of the Winthrop Glacier to Granite Creek wilderness camp, an elevation loss of 900 feet and a gain of 1100 feet. *From Granite Creek* the next campsite is 5.1 miles at Sunrise's walk-in campground. To reach it, the trail climbs 500 feet over Skyscraper Pass, traverses meadowland to Frozen Lake, and then drops to the campground. An alternative for those looking for an ice-cream cone or a hot meal is to go directly to the concession near the Sunrise parking area. Whichever trail is used, *from Sunrise* the Wonderland Trail drops 2000 feet in 3 miles to White River Campground.

Note: At times in the past, the Winthrop Creek bridge below the Winthrop Glacier has been washed out during the winter and early summer hikers have had to ford. Check with a ranger for crossing difficulties.

## PART 3: WHITE RIVER TO LONGMIRE

> **One-way trip:** 34.8 miles
> **Allow:** 4 to 6 days
> **High point:** 6700 feet
> **Elevation gain:** 5700 feet
> **Hikeable:** mid-July through September  ❸

The third and final section of the Wonderland Trail, around the east side of The Mountain and back to the starting point on the south, offers still more forests, creeks, flowers, and glaciers. It traverses the highest portion of the circuit, the most likely place of all to see mountain goats.

There are five wilderness trailside camps along the way, at 7.7 miles, 12.2 miles, 18.6 miles, 22.2 miles, and 30.3 miles.

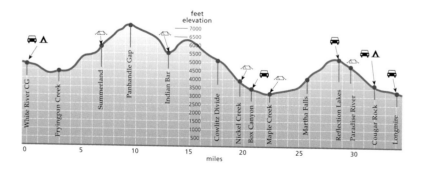

*From White River Campground* follow the trail along the campground entry road. Go right, cross the highway bridge, and walk another 300 feet to the Wonderland Trail, which parallels the highway for 2 miles and then turns away and uphill, gaining 2100 feet in 4 miles, to wilderness camps at Summerland (Hike 22), 7.7 miles from the start at White River. *From Summerland* it is another 4.5 miles to wilderness camps at Indian Bar. On the way cross high, barren Panhandle Gap (Hike 22) with a long traverse through a boulder field and snowpatches that may last through the summer, then descend to Indian Bar, an elevation gain of 800 feet and a loss of 1500 feet. If the weather is bad, one may want to consider staying an extra day at Summerland. (If the party is inexperienced or wintry conditions make it necessary or desirable to avoid Panhandle Gap, an alternate route runs from Fryingpan Creek to Box Canyon via Owyhigh Lakes, Hike 21; the East Side Trail, Hike 35; and Cowlitz Divide, Hike 40. Wilderness camps near Owyhigh Lakes at Tamanos Creek and at Deer Creek.)

*From Indian Bar* the next wilderness camp is at Nickel Creek, 6.4 miles, an elevation gain of 500 feet and a loss of 2300 feet. *From Nickel Creek* the trail crosses the Stevens Canyon Road and in 3.6 miles reaches Maple Creek wilderness camp, losing 800 feet. *From Maple Creek* the next step is 9.1 miles, gaining 2200 feet and losing 900 feet, a long, arduous, and not exactly pleasant hike to Paradise River wilderness camp. Make an early start: The heat can be unbearable; even in morning shadows the heat of the day radiates from the barren, burned-off canyon wall. Maybe the worst thing for morale is the stream of automobiles speeding along the Stevens Canyon Road, never out of sight or sound. Still, there are rewards. Sylvia Falls is a nice surprise, and so is cool and refreshing Martha Falls—actually a series of falls (the most interesting one is 300 feet above the trail). From Martha Creek the trail ascends another steep mile, crosses the road, and climbs on to Louise Lake and Reflection Lakes. For the hiker so inclined, this is the place for a sidetrip to Paradise Inn for ice cream, a steak, a bath, and a soft bed with clean sheets. Hike the road 1 mile from Reflection Lakes to the Paradise–Longmire trail. Drop along Paradise River below Narada Falls to Paradise River wilderness camp.

The last section, *from Paradise River wilderness camp,* is an easy 3.5 miles, all downhill, losing 1200 feet to Longmire. The trail follows the river under Ricksecker Point, crosses the Nisqually River near Cougar Rock Campground, and continues down to complete the loop at Longmire.

The hiker who arrives back at Longmire, having hiked 95.2 miles plus sidetrips, having gained some 20,000 feet or more in elevation, can feel proud. The accomplishment is as impressive as climbing to the summit of Rainier. In many ways the hiker has come to know The Mountain more intimately than any climber and will be most aware of the many ways in which man and The Mountain and its plants and animals are interrelated. The hiker will find, as John Muir did, that, "When we try to pick out anything by itself, we find it hitched to everything else in the universe."

## 2 | EAGLE PEAK SADDLE

**Round trip:** 7 miles
**Hiking time:** 5 hours
**High point:** 5650 feet
**Elevation gain:** 2955 feet
**Hikeable:** July to October **3**

A forest hike to a great view of Mount Rainier from a high saddle on the west end of the Tatoosh Range.

Drive from the Nisqually Entrance 6 miles to Longmire. From the National Park Inn at Longmire drive past the ranger station and residences, cross the suspension bridge over the Nisqually River, and park in front of the community house, elevation 2780 feet. Walk back up the road toward the bridge to the trailhead. Sometimes the road is closed, in which case park in the Longmire parking area. Cross the bridge and continue 200 feet to the trailhead, on the left.

Most of the hike lies in virgin forest on a wide, smooth path with an easy grade. The first mile is an aisle through a dense undercover of salal. Around 2 miles is a small stream, the last water. At about 3.3 miles, good trail ends below a high-angle meadow, which in early July explodes with flowers, the Tatoosh Range adding an inspiring backdrop for the fields of beargrass. A final steep and rocky 0.5 mile climbs to the 5700-foot saddle, where the maintained trail disappears.

Walk a short way to the right for the best view of Mount Rainier. East is the Tatoosh Range. West and down is Longmire. To the south rise Adams and St. Helens, beyond miles and miles of private tree farms and the

▲ *Red heather*

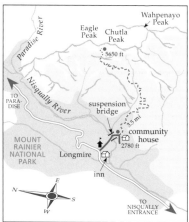

▲ *Mount Rainier from end of Eagle Peak trail*

Gifford Pinchot National Forest. Eagle Peak is very close to the park boundary, providing a good opportunity to see the difference between multiple-use lands and a "museum of primitive America."

The saddle is the essential turnaround for hikers; the final 300 feet to the summit of Eagle Peak are strictly for experienced climbers. They consider the summit ascent easy enough; the rock is solid and the ledge wide. However, the danger of a fall is great. In any event, the view from the saddle is just as good as that from the top.

# 3 | TRAIL OF THE SHADOWS

**Loop trip:** 0.7 mile
**Hiking time:** 30 minutes
**Hikeable:** two-thirds of the year   **1**

The Trail of the Shadows is a self-guiding nature walk that winds past mineral springs and a cabin built in 1888 and through a lovely cool forest.

Drive from the Nisqually Entrance 6 miles to Longmire. The trail begins directly across the highway from the National Park Inn, elevation 2750 feet. Outstanding trail features are numbered and keyed to a booklet, copies of which may be picked up at the trailhead. To follow the booklet, go counterclockwise on the loop.

The center of the loop is mostly marshy meadow with active beaver dams and numerous mineral springs, some tepid; the trail passes near two of the springs. James Longmire, on a trip to Paradise, discovered the springs, which were considerably warmer then. In 1884 he staked a mineral claim and established a hotel. The existing cabin was built by his son in 1888 on a homestead claim.

The trail continues past the cabin into dense forest. Three-fourths of the way around is the junction with the trail over Rampart Ridge (Hike 4).

Lovely in all seasons, in October the trail gives its final color show before the snows, a display of strikingly beautiful—but deadly—gold-and-orange amanita mushrooms. Remember: For all to enjoy, nothing should be removed.

## Twin Firs Loop

A grove of large trees and nurse logs, a fine example of a climax forest, on a 0.5-mile loop. Drive exactly 0.9 mile toward Longmire from the Kautz Creek bridge or 2.1 miles from Longmire toward the Nisqually Entrance to a small paved parking area and interpretive sign on the north side of the road.

The trail starts behind the twin firs, parallels the road a few feet, climbs

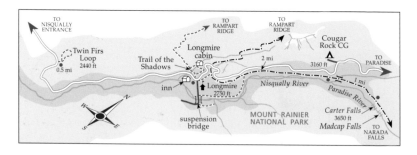

uphill crossing several small streams, and then descends and ends within a few feet of the starting point. Fallen timber makes the trail difficult to follow.

### Cougar Rock to Longmire

Drive toward Paradise to the last bend before Cougar Rock Campground and park on the wide shoulder overlooking the river. Find the trail and head downstream. The way passes through a pleasant forest between the highway and the Nisqually River, sometimes in sight of the stream. One-way distance 2 miles, all downhill.

### Carter Falls

A mile-long walk to Carter Falls on a surviving segment of the 1895 trail to Paradise Valley.

Drive toward Paradise to the last bend before Cougar Rock Campground and park on the wide shoulder overlooking the river. Cross the Nisqually River on a footbridge. The way then follows an old service road to the site of a powerhouse that occasionally supplied electricity to the park from 1924 until the late 1960s. It was removed in 1986.

The way becomes true trail. Note the old mileage markers on trees, starting with 1.8 (miles from Longmire); these were used throughout the park in the 1930s. Just above the trail is a large wooden pipeline that carried water, under pressure, to the powerhouse. At 0.7 mile note a large cedar tree with numerous woodpecker holes. It is suspected that the charred wood dates from the occasion when Longmire burned out a wasp nest that harassed his horse train. In a long mile, after a 500-foot climb, reach Carter Falls. The more photogenic Madcap Falls is only 700 feet farther.

▲ *Longmire cabin built in 1888*

# 4 | RAMPART RIDGE

**Loop trip:** 4.6 miles
**Hiking time:** 2½ hours
**High point:** 4080 feet
**Elevation gain:** 1800 feet
**Hikeable:** mid-June to October

A loop trip on excellent trail through fine forests, climbing to a cliff-edge panorama of the Nisqually River valley.

Drive to Longmire, where the hike begins and ends. It doesn't really matter which direction is taken, but by going clockwise one has glimpses of The Mountain while walking along the ridge.

Find the Trail of the Shadows nature walk directly across the road from the National Park Inn, elevation 2750 feet. Take the left (reverse) segment of the loop 800 feet, to a junction with the Rampart Ridge trail.

The wide path ascends through woods 2 miles, in a series of long switchbacks, to the ridge crest. The last switchback gives an interesting view of Tumtum Peak to the west. Then comes a cliff-top overlook of Longmire and the entire Nisqually River valley, all the way up to the buildings at Paradise.

Shortly beyond, the trail levels into a flat 0.2 mile along the ridge. When the trail drops off to the left, go straight ahead 40 feet to a grand view of The Mountain. The trail loses a few feet, crosses a rockslide, and levels off for a long 0.5 mile. At the junction with the Wonderland Trail, go right. In a bit is another junction, this time with a trail to Van Trump Park; again go

▲ *Vine maple leaves in fall color*

▲ *Looking across the Kautz Creek valley from Rampart Ridge*

right, dropping into the valley. Just before reaching Longmire the trail crosses the road; pick it up again on the far side.

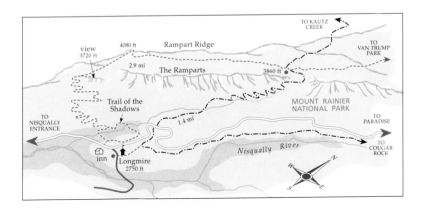

# 5 | KAUTZ CREEK

**Round trip:** 11.4 miles
**Hiking time:** 6 hours
**High point:** 5600 feet
**Elevation gain:** 2300 feet in, 200 out
**Hikeable:** mid-July to mid-October  **3**

A trail with a long history—the earliest route to Indian Henry's Hunting Ground—begins in the Kautz Creek flood area and passes through forest to the high meadow country.

Hikers on their first trip to Indian Henry's will want to save time and energy for explorations when they get there and, if the access road reopens (see Hike 6), should take the slightly shorter route with less elevation gain up Tahoma Creek. However, the Kautz Creek trail is the more interesting, giving an unusual perspective of The Mountain. If doing the hike early in the summer, make sure before starting that the footbridge is in place over Kautz Creek; high water frequently washes it away.

▲ *Kautz Creek footbridge*

*Cat tracks on
muddy beach* ▶

Drive from the Nisqually Entrance 3 miles toward Longmire and park near the nature exhibit at the Kautz Creek bridge, elevation 2378 feet. The trail starts on the opposite side of the highway.

The trail winds a short and easy way along the smooth top of the Kautz Mudflow, crosses Kautz Creek, and then enters virgin forest. The next stretch is a gentle climb, followed by a steep series of switchbacks pulling out of the valley.

In about 4 miles the trail moderates a bit and enters meadows with views south and west. Farther along, Point Success, the second-highest of Mount Rainier's three summits, can be seen poking over the ridge ahead. Early in the season there is some very muddy tread on a steep hillside. Finally the grade levels, and the last 0.7 mile traverses around the flank of Mt. Ararat and drops down to Indian Henry's. (Mount Ararat was named by Ben Longmire, who claimed to have found on this peak some petrified planks and a petrified stump with what appeared to be an old cable scar around it. Thus, this must have been where Noah's ark first touched land.)

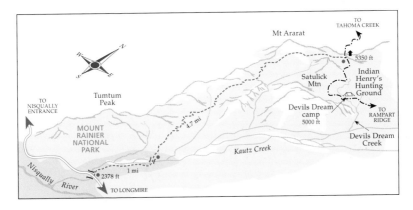

# 6 INDIAN HENRY'S HUNTING GROUND

**Round trip:** 9.5 miles (road walk 2.5 miles and trail 7 miles)
**Hiking time:** 5 hours
**High point:** 5400 feet
**Elevation gain:** 2600 feet in, 200 feet out
**Hikeable:** mid-July to mid-October

**Note:** This trail is not maintained.

One of the park's loveliest alpine meadows; in season, a blaze of flowers. A highlight is the view of Mount Rainier from Mirror Lake, a view made famous on a 1934 postage stamp. The lake is reached from a 0.7-mile spur trail that starts in the big meadow below the patrol cabin. The closest backcountry campsite is on the Wonderland Trail 1 mile east toward Longmire and 300 feet lower.

The Tahoma Creek trail used to be the most popular approach to Indian Henry's—but not since mudflows took out the good tread and closed part of the West Side Road. The Kautz Creek trail (Hike 5) is better and safer from possible outbursts from the South Tahoma Glacier.

A trail has been provided around the West Side Road washout for bicyclists to reach trailheads, but note: *Bicycles are not allowed on trails.*

Because the hillside has not stabilized since the floods, the trail has not been maintained. However, the Tahoma Creek trail is walkable by those who have sturdy shoes and don't mind vaulting a few fallen trees and scampering up a steep slippery slope or two.

From the Nisqually Entrance, drive 1 mile and go left 3.3 miles on the West Side Road and park, eleva-

◀ *Mirror Lake in Indian Henry's Hunting Ground*

tion 2850 feet, then walk the road 1.2 miles to the unmarked trailhead, elevation 3200 feet.

The trail enters woods and climbs steadily beside Tahoma Creek, sometimes at water level, sometimes 100 feet above. In about 2 miles pass a small waterfall and a few feet farther go right on the Wonderland Trail, crossing the bouncing suspension bridge.

From the bridge the trail switchbacks up old moraines to deep forest, at 3.3 miles emerging in meadows of Indian Henry's Hunting Ground, and at 3.5 miles reaching the historic patrol cabin. Asahel Curtis' famous 1934 postage stamp of Mirror Lake is on a 0.7-mile spur trail that takes off from the first meadow and wanders through flowers toward The Mountain.

Now about the gap in the West Side Road:

The recurring flash floods originating under the South Tahoma Glacier high on Mount Rainier are miniature kin to the Ice Age floods that carved the Grand Coulee region of Eastern Washington. Time after time the continental ice sheet dammed the Columbia River, and time after time the dam broke and water of the huge lake came a-whooshing oceanward, resulting in coulees of the "Channeled Scabland." On a much smaller scale, since 1986 the South Tahoma Glacier has been damming its creek, and at unpredictable times the ice has given way and loosed floods down the valley, uprooting trees, rolling house-sized boulders, and washing out a section of the West Side Road—which is repaired, then washed out, again and again. The flash floods come without warning; on occasion tourists have nearly had encounters of the Third Kind. The Mountain thus has been conceded victory in its argument with the road, which will remain closed until the glacier settles down.

The complications of the hikes to Gobblers Knob, Emerald Ridge, and Klapatche Park, formerly easy day trips, is too bad. However, the exciting presence of a Living Mountain is some compensation. St. Helens isn't the only big show in these parts.

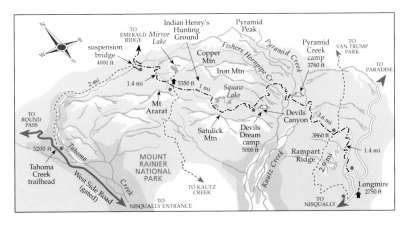

# 7 | GOBBLERS KNOB

**Round trip to Lake George:** 8.5 miles (road walk 7.5 miles
and trail 2 miles)
**Hiking time:** 5 hours
**High point:** 4300 feet
**Elevation gain:** 1900 feet
**Hikeable:** June through October **1**

**Round trip to Gobblers Knob:** 12.5 miles (road walk 7.5
miles and trail 5 miles)
**Hiking time:** 7 hours
**High point:** 5500 feet
**Elevation gain:** 2700 feet
**Hikeable:** July through mid-October **3**

A wide, well-beaten path to a mountain lake tucked away in forest and to a
fire lookout with a grand view of Tahoma Glacier and Sunset Amphitheater.

From the Nisqually Entrance, drive 1 mile and go left 3.3 miles on the
West Side Road and park, elevation 2850 feet, then walk the road 3.7 miles
to the Round Pass trailhead, elevation 3900 feet. Find the trail on the left
side of the road.

The smooth trail, probably the most popular on the west side of the
mountain, gains elevation steadily but easily, reaching Lake George in
0.9 mile. The lake, almost 0.5 mile long, is a popular campsite for both

▲ *Steller's jay*

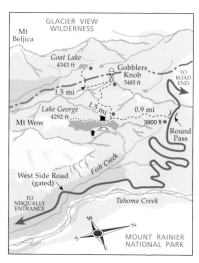

▲ *Sunset from Gobblers Knob*

fishermen and beginning hikers on their first backpack. There is a shelter—usually full. A way trail goes around the right-hand shore, to views of Mount Rainier.

The trail climbs a somewhat steeper but still quite gentle 1.5 miles from the lake to Gobblers Knob, the most northerly bump on the long ridge of Mt. Wow. A short distance below the top, a 1.5-mile sidetrail drops to Goat Lake outside the park in the Glacier View Wilderness; camping at Goat Lake, which may require a Forest Service Camping permit that is not available in the park, is more private than at Lake George. Beyond the junction the way emerges from forest to the odd and striking cliffs of the Knob, a rock garden of juniper, red heather, phlox, and other flowers in season.

The horizon from the lookout tower is all Mount Rainier on one side—but on others, St. Helens, Adams, Hood, and the Olympic Mountains. A substantial reward for a leisurely afternoon.

# 8 EMERALD RIDGE

**Round trip:** 17 miles (road walk 10 miles and trail 7 miles)
**Backpack**
**Hiking time:** 10 hours
**High point:** 5700 feet
**Elevation gain:** 2900 feet
**Hikeable:** mid-July through mid-October

Take a little-used access to the Wonderland Trail and then climb beside the Tahoma Glacier to an emerald-green ridge with a close-up look at living ice and an unique view of The Mountain.

From the Nisqually Entrance, drive 1 mile and go left 3.3 miles on the West Side Road and park, elevation 2850 feet, then walk the road 5 miles, crossing over Round Pass to the trailhead shortly before crossing the bridge over the very muddy South Puyallup River, elevation 3550 feet. One can save 0.5 mile of road walk by a short-cut trail on the right side of Round Pass.

▲ *Ptarmigan*

The trail passes through a deep forest that includes giant cedars. In 1.5 miles look for tall colonnades of columnar andesite, one of the finest examples in the park. The columns (usually hexagonal) were formed when

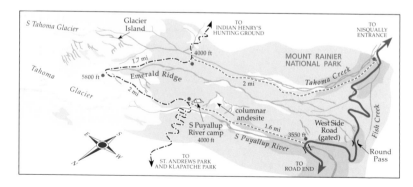

▲ *Emerald Ridge and rock-covered ice of the Tahoma Glacier*

hot lava flowed into the valley; the pattern developed as a result of shrinkage during cooling. Shortly beyond are a backcountry campsite and a junction with the Wonderland Trail. The left fork crosses the river and ascends to St. Andrews Park and Klapatche Park (Hike 9).

The right fork climbs to the ridge in about 2 miles, following old moraines and riverbeds full of cobblestones, becoming steeper but still easy enough going. Note the variety of evergreen and deciduous trees reforesting the morainal debris. As elevation is gained the Tahoma Glacier comes in sight, its flow split by Emerald Ridge into two tongues, the northeast lobe providing the source of the South Puyallup River.

The ridge top is a small, open, very green meadow, though with few flowers. Watch for goats. The "prow" of the ridge offers a splendid view up the glacier to Tokaloo Rock and the Puyallup Cleaver. To the right is the prominent cliff of Glacier Island, which until forty years ago was completely surrounded by ice; now only barren moraines are left at its base.

# 9 | KLAPATCHE PARK

**Round trip:** 21 miles (road walk 16 miles and trail 5 miles)
**Backpack**
**High point:** 5500 feet
**Elevation gain:** 2700 feet in, 200 feet out
**Hikeable:** mid-July through mid-October

An all-time favorite camp near a subalpine pond, a water-mirror ringed by soft and fragile meadows. Magnificent view of Sunset Amphitheater and dramatic sunsets. Klapatche Park can be a good overnight trip or a loop trip.

From the Nisqually Entrance, drive 1 mile and go left 3.3 miles on the West Side Road and park, elevation 2850 feet, then walk the road on foot for 8 miles, climbing over Round Pass. Lose 500 feet, then regain 300 feet to St. Andrews Creek trail, elevation 3700 feet.

The wide, smooth way climbs steadily through forest to the ridge crest, which it then follows with a few views, to a surprisingly abrupt opening into meadows at Aurora Lake at 2.5 miles. Sometimes dry in late August, the lakelet before then reflects park-land trees, towering clouds—and Mount Rainier. A few campsites are tucked in the trees on the west shore.

The sidetrip to St. Andrews Park is mandatory. Follow the Wonderland Trail uphill 0.7 mile through flower gardens, past a grand overlook of the mountain, to 6000-foot St. Andrews Lake. About the time Aurora Lake is drying up, this one is just melting out.

For an interesting loop adding 4 miles and 1500 feet elevation gain to the trip, continue walking the West Side Road another 1.2 miles to Klapatche Point, then descend 2.7 miles to campsites near the North Puyallup River bridge. Don't cross the bridge, but go right on the Wonderland Trail, climbing 1500 feet in 2.8 miles to Klapatche Park. The last 0.5 mile gives a

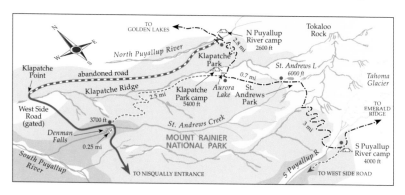

▲ *Lingering snow on the shore of Aurora Lake in Klapatche Park*

unique view of The Mountain that makes the extra effort worthwhile.

On the return trip, if time permits, be sure to take the 20-minute sidetrip from the Andrews Creek trailhead down the cool forest path 0.3 mile to Denman Falls.

To save the boredom of the road walk, an alternate route is to leave the road on the South Puyallup River Ridge trail, hike 1.5 miles to the junction of the Wonderland Trail and go left to Klapatche Park.

# 10 SUNSET PARK AND GOLDEN LAKES

**Round Trip from West Side Road**: 34 miles (road walk 18.5
  miles and trail 15.5 miles)
**Backpack**
**High Point:** 5300 feet
**Elevation gain:** 3200 feet in, 200 feet out
**Hikeable:** mid-July through mid-October ❸ ⛺

**Round trip from Mowich Lake Road:** 20 miles
**Hiking time:** 12 hours
**High point:** 5000 feet
**Elevation gain:** 2400 feet
**Hikeable:** mid-July through mid-October ❸ ⛺

The West Side Road is the closest approach to Sunset Park, but
environmental hazards associated with active volcanoes (such as the
washout, which makes the road impassable to automobiles) make the
Mowich Lake Road the quickest route.

## WEST SIDE ROAD

From the Nisqually Entrance, drive 1 mile and go left 3.3 miles on the
West Side Road and park, elevation 2850 feet, then walk the road 13 miles,
climbing over Round Pass, losing 500 feet, then regaining 300 feet to
Klapatche Point, elevation 4100 feet.

Walk the abandoned road, now a nice trail, toward The Mountain 2.7

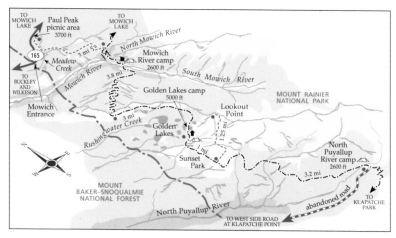

miles and join the Wonderland Trail at the crossing of the North Puyallup River. At 6.7 miles from Klapatche Point reach Sunset Park. Wander 1 mile through meadows to Golden Lakes wilderness camp.

## Mowich Lake Road

Drive via Buckley and Wilkeson on SR 165 to the Mowich Entrance and drive another 0.6 mile to the Paul Peak picnic area, elevation 3700 feet.

The trail leaves the right side of the picnic area, descends gradually, rounds Paul Peak, and at 3 miles joins the Wonderland Trail. Take the right fork, and in 0.5 mile cross a log bridge over the North Mowich River. This bridge washes out several times a year so be prepared for a difficult wade. Hike another 0.4 mile to the South Mowich River backcountry campsite, elevation 2600 feet. This camp has the only remaining trail shelter on this side of the park. This side of the mountain has so few visitors that the shelter is often vacant.

From here the trail heads upward in a series of switchbacks, climbing 2400 feet in the next 4 miles to Golden Lakes, 5000 feet.

Sidetrails lead to the lakes. For experienced off-trail hikes who want more views, continue on the Wonderland Trail another 1 mile and go up-hill at an overgrown and unsigned junctilon. The easy climb through open meadows seems to be intent on burrowing into The Mountain but in fact ends at Lookout Point, site of the former Sunset Lookout. Look up to Sunset Amphitheater and ice cliffs on Ptarmigan Ridge and down to the Golden Lakes, and out to the sunset which colors them, and afterwards to the novas of Puget Sound cities.

▲ *One of the Golden Lakes*

# 11 PAUL PEAK TRAIL

**Round trip to Mowich River shelter:** 7 miles
**Hiking time:** 4 hours
**High point:** 4200 feet
**Elevation gain:** 800 feet in, 1900 feet out
**Hikeable:** April or May through October

It is called the Paul Peak trail, but it doesn't go near the peak. This is a hike through deep timber, ideal for spring and autumn when higher trails are under snow. Short on vistas but long on virgin forest, ethereal in fall mists. Keep an eye out for mushrooms, both the safely edibles and the eyes-only.

Drive via Buckley and Wilkeson on SR 165 to the Mowich Entrance and another 0.6 mile to the Paul Peak picnic area, elevation 3700 feet.

The trail descends 250 feet from the picnic area, climbs 600 feet, then gradually rounds Paul Peak before plunging 1200 feet to join the Wonderland Trail at 3 miles. The right fork descends to the Mowich River backcountry campsite and a shelter, elevation 2600 feet.

In early summer when high trails are snowfree, a loop trip can be made by way of Mowich Lake. At the 3-mile junction go left, following the Wonderland Trail, which in 2 miles switchbacks, climbing 2000 feet from the river, then levels out to a gently climbing mile along Crater Creek to Mowich Lake and the road-end, for a total of 6.9 miles.

Rather than walk all the way back on the road, at 0.2 mile down the road from the lake find the unmaintained Grindstone Trail and use it to shortcut the long switchbacks required by passenger cars. The trail was built by Bailey Willis in 1884 and provided the first "tourist" access to Rainier's high meadowlands. Follow it 0.7 mile and rejoin the road to the starting point for a total round-trip hike of 12 miles.

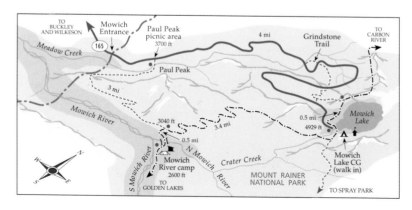

▲ *Twinflower along the Paul Peak trail*

# 12 | TOLMIE PEAK

**Round trip:** 7.2 miles
**Hiking time:** 3 hours
**High point:** 5939 feet
**Elevation gain:** 1200 feet in, 200 feet out
**Hikeable:** mid-July through September

A view supreme and a serene alpine lake. This is the peak long thought to have been climbed in 1833 by Dr. Tolmie, first European to visit what is now the park. (Recent research indicates Tolmie actually climbed Hessong Rock, closer to the mountain.)

Drive via Buckley and Wilkeson to the Mowich Entrance and continue to the road-end at Mowich Lake, elevation 4929 feet. The road is unpaved and generally rough, but passable at slow speeds.

Find the Wonderland Trail on the left side of the road just on arriving at the lake. The path skirts the forested shores on a fairly level grade, rising and falling a bit. At 1.6 miles is Ipsut Pass, where the Wonderland Trail descends right 4 miles to the Carbon River (Hike 16). Take the left fork another 1 mile to Eunice Lake, first dropping 100 feet, then turning steeply up 2.6 miles from the road.

Eunice Lake, at an elevation of 5355 feet, is one of the prettiest lakes

*Golden-mantled ground squirrel* ▶

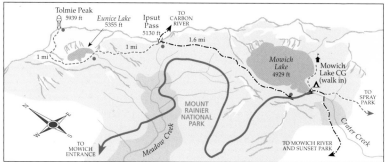

▲ *Eunice Lake and Mount Rainier*

in the park. Rising above is Tolmie Peak, the lookout cabin plainly visible. Follow the trail around the left shore and see Mount Rainier across the foreground of wind-rippling, sun-sparkling water.

The meadows around the lake are extremely fragile and should not be compelled to endure the punishment of feet. Though not the vast flower fields of Spray Park or Paradise, they display almost all the same species.

The trip is incomplete without climbing the steep but short 1 mile to the lookout. South is Mount St. Helens, west the Olympics, and north Mt. Baker. Directly below on one side is Green Lake (Hike 15), and on the other Eunice Lake, and off where the hike began, Mowich Lake. North is the immense logging scar on Cayada Creek. Southeast, of course, is The Mountain.

# 13 SPRAY PARK

**Round trip to the broad meadow under Mt. Pleasant:**
about 6 miles
**Hiking time:** 3 hours
**High point:** 5800 feet
**Elevation gain:** 2204 feet in, 300 feet out
**Hikeable:** mid-July through October

Every Rainier hiker has his favorite, but many argue this is the supreme flower garden in the park. Pond-sprinkled meadows, easy-roaming ridges, endless and delightful nooks and crannies. In the past as many as 185 campers were counted at Spray Park, with another 200 day-hikers. To let the meadows recover from years of such impact, camping is now prohibited. However, camping is allowed at Mowich Lake and Eagle's Roost Camp near Spray Falls.

Drive via Buckley and Wilkeson to the Mowich Entrance and continue to the road-end at Mowich Lake, elevation 4929 feet.

Find the Wonderland Trail near the lake outlet and descend 0.2 mile to a split. The Wonderland goes right; go left on the Spray Park trail, up a little, down a little, through subalpine forest, around the side of Fay Peak and Hessong Rock. At 1.8 miles is Eagle Cliff, a fine spot to sit for a long look at The Mountain, especially the Mowich Glacier. Past Eagle's Roost wilderness campsite, a sidetrail crosses a footlog and goes 0.25 mile to Spray Falls, a wide splash of water; only a fraction of the falls can be seen—the main part is uphill, out of sight—but what can be seen is beautiful enough.

From the falls sidetrail the main trail switchbacks steeply up some 600 feet in 0.5 mile to the lowermost meadows of Spray Park. Day-hikers often

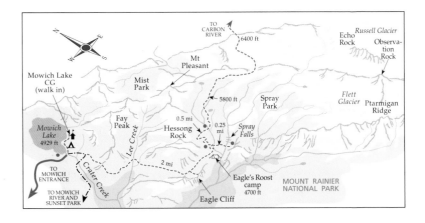

▲ *Field of avalanche lilies in fog-shrouded Spray Park*

have lunch here and turn around, well satisfied with the flowers and with the glaciers beyond 7800-foot Echo Rock and 8300-foot Observation Rock. However, the first really broad meadow, under Mt. Pleasant, is another few minutes, and the farther one goes, the better the views. Continue on the trail to the 6400-foot ridge above Seattle Park (Hike 17); on a clear day the view extends all the way beyond lower buttresses of Mount Rainier to the North Cascades.

# 14 | CARBON RIVER TRAILS

**Note:** In 1998 the Carbon River changed course, destroying the park road at Falls Creek, and the October 2003 storms caused further damage. Please contact the Park for current conditions as closures may add 3 to 5 miles each way to this hike. The Rain Forest Loop Nature Trail is not affected by the road closure.

The Olympic rain forest—that's what one is reminded of when walking in the cool, damp growth of the Carbon River valley, seeing the moss-draped trees, the soft carpet of moss on the ground, the classic examples of nurse logs, and all the thriving life in the green-gloomy understory.

Drive via Buckley and Wilkeson to the Carbon River Entrance, elevation 1750 feet. No trail runs the length of the forest but several short spurs offer easy samples.

### Rain Forest Loop Nature Trail  1

This is one of the few known inland examples of temperate rain forest, which usually occurs near the ocean coast.

On the right side of the road at the park entrance, find the self-guiding nature trail. The 0.5-mile loop leads partly through a marsh and partly through huge trees, with numbered stops discussing the rain-forest environment.

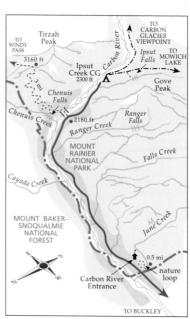

### Chenuis Falls Trail  1

At 3.5 miles from the park entrance is the Chenuis Falls trailhead on the left side of the road. The trail crosses the Carbon River on a bridge and winds through forest a short bit to the falls, which cascade down a series of rock slabs. The bridge washes out almost every spring and isn't replaced until summer, when the water recedes.

### Ipsut Falls Trail  1

At Ipsut Creek Campground at the end of the Carbon River road, 5 miles from the park entrance, follow

▲ *Rain forest nature trail*

the Wonderland Trail south toward Mowich Lake 0.3 mile. Just before the trail begins its uphill climb, take a sidetrail right a few hundred feet to a view of the falls.

### Carbon Glacier Viewpoint

This is the most popular hike in the valley, to a viewpoint close to the snout of the Carbon Glacier. Most of the way is in forest with occasional views of Mount Rainier. The trail crosses the Carbon River on a swaying suspension bridge that scares off some hikers. If the lower bridge is in place, it provides an alternate route easier on the nerves.

From the Ipsut Creek Campground, hike upstream as described in Hike 17. At 2 miles, if the lower bridge is in place, go left for the alternate route. Otherwise continue a mile to the suspension bridge across the Carbon River. A short distance beyond the crossing, turn uphill and go 0.2 mile to the viewpoint. Don't be tempted to approach the glacier face; boulders frequently melt out and come bouncing down.

# 15 GREEN LAKE

**Round trip:** 4 miles
**Hiking time:** 2 hours
**High point:** 3185 feet
**Elevation gain:** 1200 feet
**Hikeable:** May to November

**Note:** In 1998 the Carbon River changed course, destroying the park road at Falls Creek, and the October 2003 storms caused further damage. Contact the Park for current information; closures may add 3 to 5 miles each way to the hike.

In a national park with many wonderful forest trails, this walk to a crystal-clear lake stands far above all the rest.

Drive 3 miles beyond the Carbon River Entrance to a small parking space at the Ranger Creek crossing (a culvert), elevation 985 feet. The trail is on the right.

The beginning is a climb through a grove of giant trees, centuries old. During the first 0.5 mile the floor is rich in ferns and devil's club. One gnarled root system would serve as a proper throne for a forest prince. Above the path are numerous tree bridges—overpasses for squirrels, no doubt.

In 1 mile take a short sidetrip to Ranger Creek Falls. In 1.5 miles the path levels and crosses the creek and at 2 miles reaches the lake, deep in lush forest. (Because of extreme fire hazard in the forest duff, and the large number of visitors who easily could "love the lake to death," camping is not permitted.)

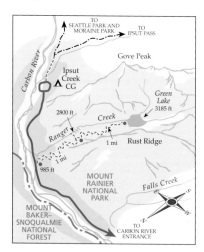

▲ *Oak ferns*

*Ranger Creek Falls* ▶

# 16 IPSUT CREEK

**Round trip:** 8 miles
**Hiking time:** 4 hours
**High point:** 5100 feet
**Elevation gain:** 2800 feet
**Hikeable:** June through October

**Note:** In 1998 the Carbon River changed course, destroying the park road at Falls Creek, and the October 2003 storms caused further damage. Contact the Park for current information; closures may add 3 to 5 miles each way to the hike.

A forested segment of the Wonderland Trail passing the world's largest known Alaska yellow-cedar. The woods walk as far as the big tree is pleasant in itself, particularly early in the season when the high country is buried in snow.

Drive to the Carbon River Entrance and go 5 miles to the road-end at Ipsut Creek Campground, elevation 2300 feet. The trail starts at the upper end of the camping area, follows the dirt road 300 feet, and turns right at a prominent sign in a few more feet to join the Wonderland Trail. Go right, and in a short distance climbing begins. The path is wide and mostly smooth. The trees are impressively tall, and the ground is carpeted with moss and flowers. The trail continues steadily upward, crossing numerous small streams. Ipsut Creek is a constant roar on the right.

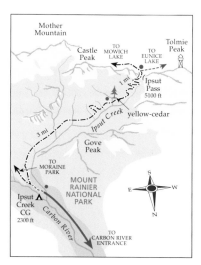

▲ *Clark's nutcracker*

▲ *Headwall of Ipsut Creek Valley*

In about 3 miles the way emerges from forest and crosses the creek, which though still noisy is now only a step wide. The specimen cedar is in a grove of subalpine trees just beyond the crossing. Actually, after the huge firs and hemlocks lower down, the largest Alaska yellow-cedar in the world doesn't look very impressive. However, many hundreds of years are required for that species to attain such size.

The cedar is a good turnaround. Above here the way steepens to a series of short switchbacks as it works its way between towering cliffs to 5100-foot Ipsut Pass. The most notable spot is a free shower from a waterfall under a tall cliff overhanging the trail.

This route is an alternate way to Tolmie Peak or Mowich Lake (Hike 12). From Ipsut Pass, Mowich Lake is 1.6 miles to the left and Tolmie Peak 2 miles to the right.

# 17 | SEATTLE PARK

**Round trip to Seattle Park:** 12 miles
**Hiking time:** 7 hours
**High point:** 5200 feet
**Elevation gain:** 3000 feet
**Hikeable:** mid-July to mid-October

**Round trip to divide:** 16 miles
**Allow:** 2 days
**High point:** 6400 feet
**Elevation gain:** 4200 feet
**Hikeable:** mid-July to mid-October

**Note:** In 1998 the Carbon River changed course, destroying the park road at Falls Creek, and the October 2003 storms caused further damage. Contact the Park for current information; closures may add 3 to 5 miles each way to the hike.

A picturelike parkland of heather meadows interspersed with groves of subalpine trees. There are no campsites in Seattle Park, making it a long and very strenuous day hike from the road. However, camping is permitted at two closer spots.

From the Carbon River Entrance drive 5 miles to the road-end at Ipsut Creek Campground, elevation 2300 feet.

Find the trail at the upper boundary of the camp. In 0.2 mile stay left and

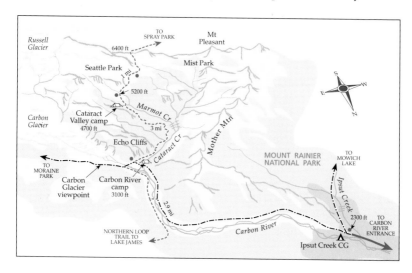

▲ *Echo Rock (left) and Observation Rock (right) from Seattle Park*

join the Wonderland Trail. Hike the easy grade partly on a long-abandoned road up the west side of the Carbon River, at 2 miles passing a trail that goes left across the river. Continue straight ahead to Carbon River wilderness camp and Cataract Creek junction at 2.9 miles; go right.

Now come 3 miles of steady climbing, at 4.5 miles from the road passing Cataract Valley wilderness camp to the first open meadow. Except for the last 0.5 mile the trail in the forest is nicely graded. At 6 miles from the road, on the edge of meadowland, is Marmot Creek, elevation 5200 feet, the usual turnaround. To fully appreciate the wide-open country of Seattle Park, continue at least another 0.5 mile or, better yet, 2 more miles, crossing permanent snowfields and topping the 6400-foot ridge above Spray Park (Hike 13).

# 18 | MORAINE PARK—MYSTIC LAKE

**Round trip to Mystic Lake:** 15.6 miles
**Hiking time:** 8 hours
**High point:** 6004 feet
**Elevation gain:** 3800 feet in, 400 out
**Hikeable:** mid-July to October

**Note:** In 1998 the Carbon River changed course, destroying the park road at Falls Creek, and the October 2003 storms caused further damage. Contact the Park for current information; closures may add 3 to 5 miles each way to the hike.

A close look at the snout of the Carbon Glacier, lowest-elevation glacier in the old 48 states, flower meadows and high ridges for roaming, and a near view of enormous Willis Wall. If lucky, one may see avalanches seemingly float down the 3600-foot cliff.

Drive to the Carbon River Entrance and another 5 miles to the road-end at Ipsut Creek Campground, elevation 2300 feet. Find the trail at the upper boundary of the camp. In 0.2 mile go left on the Wonderland Trail.

The first 3 miles follow the valley above the river. Pass the Northern Loop junction at 2 miles and Carbon River Camp and Seattle Park junction at a scant 3 miles; shortly beyond cross the Carbon River on a suspension bridge that makes some hikers turn pale and lose their knees. If the sway is too much for the nerves, go back to the Northern Loop Trail, cross the river on a log bridge, and hike up the far bank. A short distance beyond the suspension bridge is a junction; go right, uphill.

The trail steepens, gaining 1700 feet in 2 miles. In 0.4 mile pass a striking viewpoint of the Carbon Glacier snout. Though some other glaciers in

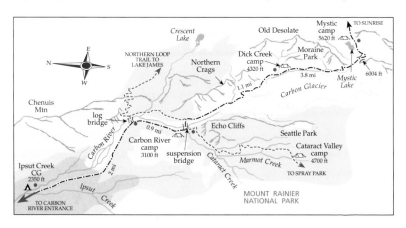

▲ *Wonderland Trail traversing Moraine Park*

the park have receded almost a mile in the last thirty years, the Carbon has held its own. The next 0.4 mile is very rough, crossing rubbly, cliffy slopes hanging above the ice, but provides more views of the snout. In another mile is tumbling Dick Creek, a good rest stop; just beyond is Dick Creek wilderness camp. The trail enters forest and smooths out, though it's still steep. The final stretch emerges in parkland and flattens.

Officially, Moraine Park is out of sight high above the trail, but hikers generally refer to all the tree-and-flower slopes of lower Curtis Ridge as Moraine Park. The official Moraine Park is pretty enough, especially in flower season, but the best is farther ahead. Follow the trail up a steep mile to a 6004-foot saddle. A short drop leads to Mystic Lake and camps.

# 19 | WINDY GAP—NATURAL BRIDGE

**Round trip:** 16 miles
**Hiking time:** 9 hours
**High point:** 5800 feet
**Elevation gain:** 3500 feet in, 300 feet out
**Hikeable:** mid-July to mid-October

**Note:** In 1998 the Carbon River changed course, destroying the park road at Falls Creek, and the October 2003 storms caused further damage. Contact the Park for current information; closures may add 3 to 5 miles each way to the hike.

Hike a portion of the Northern Loop Trail to colorful cliffs, arctic-like tundra, and a natural bridge on Independence Ridge. What with road-walking, the hike is too much for a day and is recommended as a backpack.

Drive to the Carbon River Entrance and another 5 miles to the road-end at Ipsut Creek Campground, elevation 2300 feet.

Find the Wonderland Trail at the upper boundary of the camp. The first 2 miles follow the valley above the river. At a junction take the left fork across the Carbon River. The river often floods and frequently changes course, washing out the bridge; the exact point of crossing therefore varies. On the far side of the river is a split. The right fork heads upstream toward Moraine Park; turn left and follow the Northern Loop Trail.

The way goes down the valley a bit, then begins an unrelenting 3000-foot, 4-mile climb to Windy Gap. The first 3 miles are through forest on a smooth and soft path. At 3.8 miles from Ipsut Creek Campground is

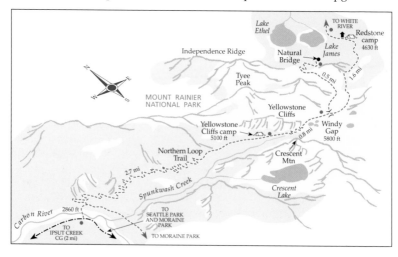

▲ *Natural Bridge overlooking Ethel Lake (left) and Lake James*

Yellowstone Cliffs wilderness camp. The final 0.7 mile tends to be muddy
and becomes an endless stairway, but the great meadows compensate for
any muss. The trail rounds beneath Tyee Peak and the Yellowstone Cliffs
and passes three shallow lakes before coming to 5800-foot Windy Gap, 6
miles from the road-end.

Continue over the pass a short distance to a fork. Straight ahead, the
Northern Loop Trail descends 2 miles to campsites at Lake James; go left,
contouring 0.5 mile across the open slopes of Independence Ridge, in views
to Fremont Lookout and Grand Park. Then switchback downhill, losing
200 feet, to a viewpoint of Natural Bridge, awkwardly located for a really
good photograph but spectacular all the same—about 100 feet high and
100 feet long, it arches over a deep ravine, appearing to defy gravity.

# 20 | NORTHERN LOOP TRAIL

**Round trip:** 37 miles
**Hiking time:** 4 days
**High point:** 6740 feet
**Elevation gain:** 8500 feet
**Hikeable:** mid-July to mid-October ❸ △

**Note:** In 1998 the Carbon River changed course, destroying the park road at Falls Creek, and the October 2003 storms caused further damage. Contact the Park for current information; closures may add 3 to 5 miles each way to the hike.

A long loop hike in the most pristine wilderness of the park, through forests and meadows, over rivers, under a cliff of colorful rocks, near Natural Bridge, past numerous mountain lakes, in ever-changing views of The Mountain and its glaciers. The first portion to Lake James can be done as an overnight trip.

Drive to the Carbon River Entrance and another 5 miles to the road-end at Ipsut Creek Campground, elevation 2300 feet.

Find the Wonderland Trail at the upper boundary of the camp. The first 2 miles follow the valley above the river. At a junction take the left fork across the Carbon River (Hike 19). On the far bank turn left again, downstream a bit. Then begins a series of countless switchbacks, climbing 3000 feet, mostly—a mercy—in cool forest on a smooth and soft path. At 6.7 miles from Ipsut Creek Campground pass Yellowstone Cliffs wilderness camp. Above the trail are Tyee Peak and the Yellowstone Cliffs; beside it, a pair of small lakes to the left and another to the right. The tundra of 5800-foot Windy Gap (6 miles from Ipsut Creek) offers wide views, well worth a lengthy lunch stop.

◀ *Lunch break at Windy Pass*

A few hundred yards beyond the top of Windy Gap is the sidetrail to Natural Bridge, a 1.7-mile round trip (Hike 19).

The Northern Loop Trail descends 1400 feet in 2 miles to camps at Lake James, 4370 feet. Here, 8 miles from Ipsut Creek, is the turnaround for overnighters. (If Lake James is the aim, it's better to start at Sunrise, the distance being less.)

From Lake James the route drops to a crossing of the West Fork White River, where a 2500-foot climb begins, at 4.2 miles passing a sidetrail to Fire Creek wilderness camp. Water is not dependable here; if camping is the plan, fill buckets at Van Horn Falls, near the West Fork. At 6 miles from Lake James is a junction with the Grand Park trail (Hike 29). Continue right another 4.6 miles to a camp in lower Berkeley Park. Total distance from Lake James, 9 miles.

From Berkeley Park wilderness camp climb 1.2 miles through meadows to a junction with the Wonderland Trail. Turn right and cross 6740-foot Skyscraper Pass. Descend 800 feet to Granite Creek wilderness camp, 4.5 miles from Berkeley Park. From Skyscraper Pass the trail drops a total of 2100 feet to the snout of the Winthrop Glacier and a crossing of Winthrop Creek, a tributary of the White River, then gains 1200 feet to Mystic wilderness camp at 5620 feet, 10 miles from Berkeley Park.

To complete the remaining 8 miles of the loop, the trail climbs 400 feet to a 6100-foot pass and then (as described in Hike 18) descends through Moraine Park, crosses the Carbon River, and returns to the trail start at Ipsut Creek and back to the park entrance.

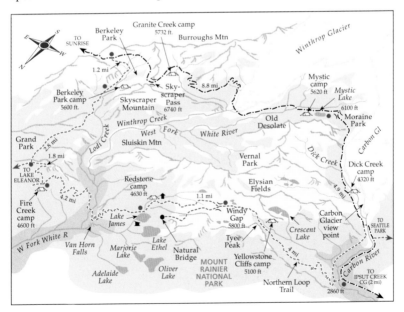

# 21 OWYHIGH LAKES

**Round trip to lakes from White River:** 7 miles
**Hiking time:** 3½ hours
**High point:** 5185 feet
**Elevation gain:** 1350 feet
**Hikeable:** mid-July through October

Alpine lakes surrounded by acres of wildflowers in the shadow of the ragged peaks of Governors Ridge.

There are two ways to reach the lakes: a 3.5-mile trail from the White River road, and a 5-mile trail from the road to Ohanapecosh. If transportation can be arranged, the two can be combined in a one-way hike; the best starting place for such a trip is the White River approach, since going this direction involves slightly less elevation gain.

Drive from the White River Entrance 2 miles to a parking area on the right, 1 mile beyond Shaw Creek, elevation 3750 feet.

The trail starts on the left side of the road and climbs steadily through the woods, the path wide and smooth with long switchbacks. At 3 miles, 0.5 mile short of the lakes, is Tamanos Creek wilderness camp, the only camp on this trail. Tamanos Creek normally is dry by mid-August. The timber thins shortly before reaching the 5100-foot lakes. There is no access trail to the lakes. Enjoy the view from the trail. To the east is craggy Governors Ridge. Directly west is Tamanos Mountain.

From the lakes the trail climbs another 300 feet to a 5400-foot pass with a view of the Cowlitz Chimneys, then drops steadily but not steeply into Kotsuck Creek valley and down to the junction with the East Side Trail. In

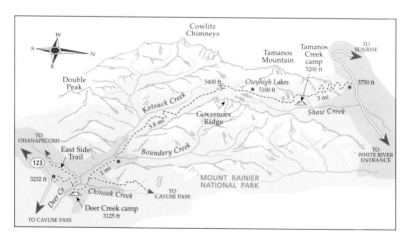

▲ *Owyhigh Lakes and one of the Cowlitz Chimneys*

about 2 miles pass a viewpoint of a waterfall. In 3 miles cross Boundary Creek. Take time out to walk up the creek bed to a waterfall.

Save energy for the last 0.5 mile. At the junction with the East Side Trail, cross Chinook Creek, then Deer Creek, and take the Deer Creek trail, which climbs 360 feet to the highway.

# 22 SUMMERLAND

**Round trip:** 8.4 miles
**Hiking time:** 4 hours
**High point:** 5920 feet
**Elevation gain:** 2100 feet
**Hikeable:** July to October

One of the favorite hikes in the park, on a wide path to an alpine meadow under the pinnacle of Little Tahoma. For those who don't wish to do the whole trip, the lower portion of the trail makes a fine forest walk. Many deep-woods flowers that by early summer have come and gone on the south side of the park are just starting to bloom in this valley as late as the middle of August; especially notable is the queen's cup beadlily. This is one of the most crowded areas of the park, with 100 to 200 hikers a day.

Drive from the White River Entrance 3 miles to a parking area just beyond the Fryingpan Creek bridge, elevation 3800 feet.

The trail starts across the highway and in 0.1 mile joins the Wonderland Trail. For 2 miles the way ascends gently in forest to an overlook of thundering Fryingpan Creek. At about 3 miles pass through debris of a large avalanche and cross the creek. The final 1 mile is steep, ending in a series of short switchbacks; here, during July and August, look for attractive displays of avalanche lilies.

The stone shelter cabin and wilderness campsites are in the grove to the left. Little Tahoma dominates the meadows, rising above the Fryingpan Glacier to the southwest. West are the Emmons Glacier and Mount Rainier. North is Goat Island Mountain. East are the Sarvent Glaciers. South is Panhandle Gap.

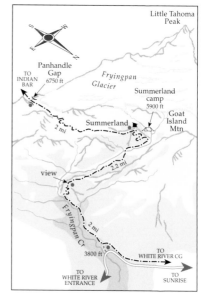

If transportation can be arranged, and one of the very limited backcountry camping permits obtained, a classic 2- to 3-day trip is over Panhandle Gap to Indian Bar (Hike 41) and on down to Box Canyon on the Stevens Canyon Road, a total one-way distance of 17 miles.

From Summerland climb 840 feet in less than 2 miles to 6750-foot

Panhandle Gap. A good share of this distance is through rough moraine. From the Gap the trail traverses wintry and barren slopes above Ohanapecosh Park 1.5 miles before descending 2 miles to Indian Bar. This is the highest and most desolate section of the Wonderland Trail. Much of the way lies over large snowfields; though the route is marked by a few rock cairns, it is very easy to lose in a fog, not to mention a storm. Inexperienced hikers should not attempt to travel this area early in the season or in bad weather. After spells of good weather, though, generally the track is clearly booted into the snow and probably can be followed even in a dense fog.

From Indian Bar proceed on out the Cowlitz Divide to Box Canyon. Panhandle Gap demands a special note. Atop the Gap, look up and left to the Cowlitz Chimneys, volcanic plugs from old eruptions; except on very hot days, there is a fair chance of seeing mountain goats.

◄ *Red monkey-flowers* (Mimulus lewisii) *line a small stream*

# 23 | GLACIER BASIN

**Round trip:** 6 miles
**Hiking time:** 4 hours
**High point:** 6000 feet
**Elevation gain:** 1704 feet
**Hikeable:** July to October

A trip that offers no overwhelming view of The Mountain (The Wedge is in the way), but more than compensates with the peaceful seclusion of a meadowy basin. The easy walk also displays artifacts of the Storbo Mine. From here, in 1894–5, "high-grading" prospectors took out ore samples worth $450 a ton—had there been a ton. In 1902 a copper claim was established, but despite sporadic speculative activity until 1957, nothing of commercial value was ever found.

Drive from the White River Entrance 5 miles to the White River bridge and turn left on the road to White River Campground. Find the trail at the upper end of the camp, elevation 4350 feet.

The walking begins—and continues much of the way—on remnants of the miners' old wagon road, which was passable to automobiles as late as

▲ *Marmot and Glacier Basin trail*

the 1940s. The open road is hot on sunny days but runs close to cool pools of the Inter Fork of the White River.

At 1 mile is a junction with the Emmons Moraine trail, a 0.5-mile sidetrip to a view of the snout of the largest glacier in the conterminous 48 states. One must use imagination to be properly impressed by the heaps of rubble covering the glacial ice, much of it from a 1980s massive slide off of Little Tahoma. There is, however, a good view of Little Tahoma rising above. In 2.5 miles pass the remains of the miners' sawmill and power plant. Here the trail leaves what's left of the mine road and climbs steeply into open meadows, then levels off and enters Glacier Basin.

▲ *Avalanche lily pushing its way through last winter's snowbank*

Bands of goats prowl the high slopes. In season the basin floor is bright with flowers. A tiny bit of The Mountain appears above The Wedge, topped by Mt. Ruth and Steamboat Prow. Splendid campsites.

A climbers' track continues from the basin toward Interglacier, rising out of flowers and greenery into bouldery wastes of ice country.

If transportation can be arranged, Glacier Basin can be reached by an easy downhill trail from Sunrise (Hike 31), one-way hikers then going on out to White River Campground.

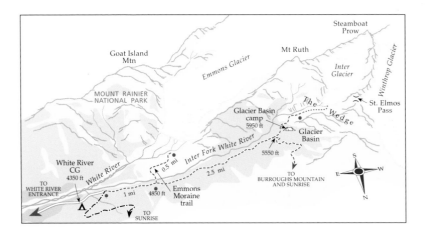

# 24 | PALISADES LAKES

**Round trip:** 7.5 miles
**Hiking time:** 4 hours
**High point:** 6150 feet
**Elevation gain:** 700 feet in, 900 feet
**Hikeable:** mid-July to mid-October

A series of at least seven lakes along the trail, all on the "dry" side of the mountain. No views of The Mountain, but an interesting rock formation called The Palisades. The trail has a bad feature: It drops 500 feet and then goes up and down, up and down.

Drive from the White River Entrance 10.5 miles to the parking area at Sunrise Point. Cross the highway to the north side and look over the

▲ *Clover Lake*

stone railing directly down at Sunrise Lake, the first of the series. The trail starts at the north end of the horseshoe bend in the road, elevation 6150 feet.

The way follows the ridge down a short distance, then switchbacks toward Sunrise Lake. In 0.5 mile the trail divides. The left fork leads to Sunrise Lake, the choice of most hikers and a good destination for a short walk. However, more and better lakes lie beyond, so take the right fork.

In 1.5 miles from the road the path skirts Clover Lake, largest of the chain. At 2.5 miles pass Tom, Dick, and Harry Lakes (campsite at Dick) and a sidetrail to Hidden Lake. The main trail ends in another mile at Upper Palisades Lake.

▲ *Sunrise Lake*

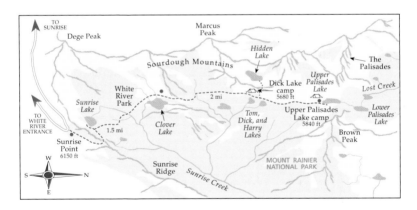

## 25 | SUNRISE NATURE TRAILS

**Round trip:** 1 to 4 miles
**Hikeable:** mid-July through September

A glacier overlook, a walk high above the White River through a silver forest with views directly down on White River Campground, and a gem of a lake. Drive from the White River Entrance to Sunrise and take as many of these hikes as time and energy permit.

▲ *Indian paintbrush and Emmons Glacier from Silver Forest trail*

## Sourdough Ridge Nature Trail 🆔

A self-guiding nature trail, starting on the north side of the picnic area and going in a loop, an easy hour's stroll, through meadows and along the ridge to fine views of Rainier and down to Huckleberry Park.

## Emmons Vista Nature Trail 🆔

Find the 0.5-mile trail directly across the parking lot from Sunrise Lodge, near the gravel road to the campground. At the start is a box containing copies of an interpretive pamphlet keyed to numbered posts along the way. At the end of the trail is an exhibit explaining the workings of a glacier.

## Silver Forest 🆔

From Sunrise walk the Emmons Vista Nature Trail a short bit to the start of the Silver Forest trail. The way is fairly level, traversing the brow of the hill above the White River valley. Views of The Mountain are unlimited; the silver forest, trees killed by fire and bleached by weather, offers picturesque foregrounds. Mountain bluebirds make their homes in the snags.

## Sunrise Rim Trail 🆔

At a junction in the Emmons Vista Nature Trail, turn right and contour along a steep hillside with views of The Mountain and White River. Pass a junction with the Wonderland Trail which drops 3 miles to the White River. Shadow Lake is surrounded by groves of alpine trees and flowers in season. Views of Little Tahoma, though Mount Rainier is hidden. The hike-in campground is near the lake. Return by either of two trails.

A considerably more energetic (but worth it) alternate return is via the high trail visible up on the Sourdough Mountains. Follow the Wonderland Trail upward (west) from the campground, climbing steeply to Frozen Lake, the fenced water supply for facilities at Sunrise. After climbing 500 feet in less than 0.5 mile, leave the Wonderland Trail and pass below the lake. Walk a long 1 mile over a hump and along a sidehill, then drop through meadows to Sunrise.

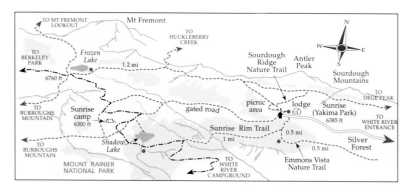

# 26 | SOURDOUGH TRAIL

**Round trip:** 4 miles
**Hiking time:** 2 hours
**High point:** 7006 feet
**Elevation gain:** 600 feet
**Hikeable:** mid-July through September ▮**1**

An alpine ridge with a classic view of Mount Rainier. Look down on Sunrise Lodge and the busy highway. End at the Sunrise Point parking lot. Along the way take a spur trail to the top of Dege Peak for a broad panorama of Cascade Crest summits.

Drive from the White River Entrance to Sunrise, elevation 6385 feet.

The Sourdough Mountains are the long ridge of low peaks rising to the north. The trail leaves from the picnic area at a large sign. In a short distance pass a junction. Keep right, following signs for Dege Peak. Soon the trail is joined by a slash in the meadow, a steep eroded shortcut from the lodge built over the years by boots of countless impatient hikers. Thousands of hours of work by rangers and the Youth Conservation Corps have gone into rehabilitating the shortcut, replanting and restoring it to meadow.

The views get better and the crowds thinner the farther one goes out the ridge. The path stays near the crest, contouring around the higher summits. Where the track starts up Dege Peak, keep left at a junction for the final short bit to the top.

Horizons are limitless. Mount Rainier is supreme, of course, but cannot deny the Sarvent Glaciers and Cowlitz Chimneys to the south. Far below is the White River and SR 410, the highway over Chinook Pass. Farther north rise distant peaks of the Cascades and northwest are the Olympic Mountains. At the east base of the peak lie Sunrise and Clover Lakes (Hike 24), and on the northwest slopes are the green meadows of Huckleberry Park.

If transportation can be arranged, go back the short bit to the junction

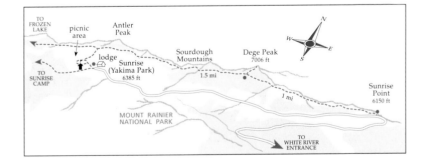

▲ *Highway to Sunrise Visitor Center from Sourdough Mountain trail*

and take the trail 1 mile down the ridge to Sunrise Point. However, if such an opportunity is available, it's more interesting to walk from Sunrise Point to Sunrise; this way the view is always in front of you. The trail starts on the uphill side of the highway from the parking area and follows the ridge. The Sunrise Point beginning adds 300 feet of elevation to the climb but the one-way hiking distance is only 3 miles instead of the 4-mile round trip from Sunrise Lodge.

# 27 | HUCKLEBERRY CREEK

**One-way trip:** 8.7 miles
**Hiking time (downhill):** 4 hours
**High point:** 6709 feet
**Elevation gain:** 200 feet, loss 3609 feet
**Hikeable:** mid-July through September

Miles of forest walking in sound of bubbling Huckleberry Creek, passing by numerous waterfalls, Forest Lake amid the trees, and finally a meadow basin and alpine ridge—a superb approach from low country to high country and one of the wildest and most respectful ways to experience the park from bottom to top.

The trail (which probably predates the park) was built by men in a hurry to get where they wanted to go, and the upper half is very steep. Therefore, many hikers prefer to have their dessert first and then the main course and the soup and salad—which is to say, they start at the top in Yakima Park and descend to the bottom at the Huckleberry Creek road in Mount Baker–

▲ *Huckleberry Creek trail*

Snoqualmie National Forest. Whether doing the whole hike or not, don't miss the fairly level lower 2.5 miles on one of the park's finest forest trails.

From Enumclaw on SR 410, drive 6.6 miles past the town of Greenwater. Shortly after the Mount Rainier Viewpoint interpretive sign, turn right on Forest Service road No. 73, following Huckleberry Creek upstream. In the first 2 miles there is a confusion of sideroads; be careful to stay on road No. 73. At 6 miles, just before reaching the concrete Huckleberry Creek bridge, is the trailhead, elevation 3000 feet. Find Forest Service trail No. 1182 beside the stream. A sign, "Huckleberry Creek Trail—National Park Boundary 1½ Miles," may be missing.

The trail starts on a jeep track and soon becomes a true trail, crosses Lost Creek, and enters the magnificent forest.

If a one-way trip is planned, drive the second car via the White River Entrance to Sunrise, elevation 6385 feet. Walk from the picnic area, as for Mount Fremont Lookout (Hike 28), 0.5 mile to the ridge crest and turn left several hundred feet to a junction. Go right, climbing a few feet, then drop rapidly in short switchbacks to a divide between an attractive meadow basin on the right and a cold and rocky cirque on the left. The trail switchbacks down into the cirque, crosses a tumbling headwater of Huckleberry Creek, swings around a shoulder to a second headwater, then falls to forest and 5653-foot Forest Lake, with one wilderness campsite.

The grade moderates a bit below the lake but the next 3 miles still are pretty stiff. The lower reaches of the trail follow creek meanders along the valley bottom. At the park boundary is an old patrol cabin; one year this relic of the past will be the target of a toppling tree.

The bottom-to-top-and-back-again round-trip 20 miles can be done without special transportation arrangements on a weekend backpack. Those who earn the high meadows by hiking the valley approach get some notion of how glorious it was to enter Yakima Park when it was wild; they pity travelers who arrive in automobiles.

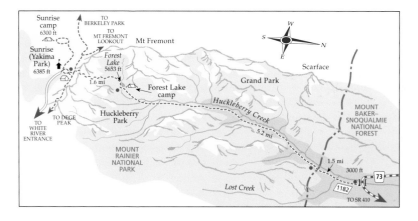

# 28 | MOUNT FREMONT LOOKOUT

**Round trip:** 5.2 miles
**Hiking time:** 3 hours
**High point:** 7200 feet
**Elevation gain:** 800 feet
**Hikeable:** mid-July through September

A fire lookout with the white glaciers of Mount Rainier on one side and the greenery of national park and national forest trees on the other.

Drive from the White River Entrance to Sunrise, elevation 6385 feet.

From the picnic area walk the Sourdough Ridge Trail upward and go left to Frozen Lake and a conjunction of five trails at 1.2 miles. The lookout trail follows the west side of Frozen Lake and climbs around the hill to the north. The highest point of the trail is at the ridge corner. From here the way descends a bit as it traverses to the lookout, which is not on the summit of Mt. Fremont.

South is The Mountain, north the long line of Cascades. On a clear day the Olympics appear, and with binoculars one can see the Space Needle in Seattle.

Closer are the flat expanse of Grand Park (Hike 30) and, beyond, the forests. Logging roads have been built by the Forest Service to the park boundary; eventually the only virgin forest remaining will be that within the park.

The lookout is occupied during periods of extreme fire danger. If a ranger is available, he or she will be glad to explain duties and show how the fire-locator works. Ask the ranger to point out Natural Bridge on the Northern Loop (Hike 19); it appears quite small from here, but is visible when the sun is right.

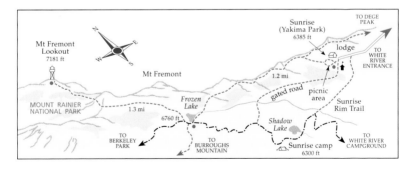

▲ *Mount Rainier from Mount Fremont Lookout*

*Band of mountain goats above Mount Fremont Lookout trail near Frozen Lake watershed fence* ▶

# 29

# SKYSCRAPER PASS—
# BERKELEY PARK

**Round trip to Skyscraper Pass:** 6.2 miles
**Hiking time:** 4 hours
**High point:** 6773 feet
**Elevation gain:** 990 feet in, 300 feet out

Round trip to Berkeley Park: **6.2 miles**
**Hiking time:** 6 hours
**High point:** 6773 feet
**Elevation gain:** 400 feet in, 1200 feet out
**Hikeable:** mid-July through September

Choose between flower-rich Berke-ley Park and cliff-ringed camping along Lodi Creek, or meadow miles of the Wonderland Trail climbing to Skyscraper Pass. Or choose both— both destinations can be done on a backpack. Bevies of blossoms, yes, but they must compete with views north along the Cascades and the bits and pieces of Mount Rainier poking above surrounding ridges.

Drive from the White River En-trance to the road-end at Sunrise, elevation 6385 feet.

From the picnic area follow the

▲ *Mountain goat*

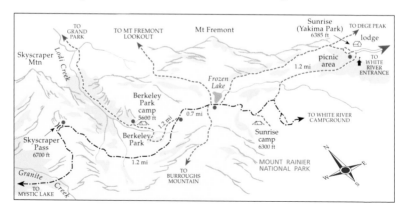

▲ *Wonderland Trail near Skyscraper Pass*

Sourdough Ridge trail upward 0.5 mile and then go left toward Frozen Lake (a reservoir). Five different trails come together near the lake; go straight on the Wonderland Trail, headed west toward Mystic Lake and the Carbon River.

From Frozen Lake the way descends 0.7 mile in 300 feet to a junction with the Northern Loop–Berkeley Park trail. For Berkeley Park go right, leaving the Wonderland Trail and dropping another 500 feet in 1.2 miles to campsites in lush greenery of trees and meadows and brilliant spottings of flowers. For Skyscraper Pass stay left on the Wonderland Trail for 1.5 miles, contouring high above Berkeley Park, then climbing to views from the 6700-foot pass: down Granite Creek to the snout of the Winthrop Glacier, across the valley to Old Desolate and Sluiskin Mountain, and to green meadows of remote, seldom-visited Vernal Park.

At the pass, pumice soils are extremely fragile and the vegetation scarce. The storm-stunted trees are hung with white left by mountain goats pushing through the branches to groom themselves.

# 30 | GRAND PARK

**Round trip:** 13.6 miles
**Hiking time:** 6 hours
**High point:** 6770 feet
**Elevation gain:** 700 feet in, 1500 out
**Hikeable:** mid-July through September

In the up-and-down landscape of Mount Rainier, the almost flat 2-mile-long plateau of Grand Park is a striking oddity. The explanation: Many millennia ago a lava flow filled an ancient canyon; the displaced streams sought new courses at the edges of the flow, leaving the lava surface as a high tableland, which was later covered by a thick layer of pumice. A small herd of elk makes its home here, and chances are good of seeing a genuinely "wild" (unaccustomed to humans) bear. For an immense display of flowers make this hike in late July.

Drive from the White River Entrance to Sunrise, elevation 6385 feet.

From the picnic area, follow the Sourdough Ridge trail, each junction keeping left. At 1.2 miles reach Frozen Lake and a five-way junction. Take the Wonderland Trail west, across and down a pretty and varied series of meadows. In 0.7 mile is another junction. Keep right and follow the Northern Loop Trail, dropping rapidly into Berkeley Park (Hike 29). Pass a series of springs (oozing ground, green lush plants). At 4 miles from Sunrise is Berkeley Park wilderness campsite. In lower Berkeley Park are loud and lovely waterfalls of Lodi Creek and a talus where marmots perch atop boulders whistling you by.

The way descends in forest to 5200 feet, a total elevation loss from Frozen Lake of 1500 feet, which must be regained on the return. Then the trail swings out of the valley onto a dividing ridge between trees of Lodi Creek

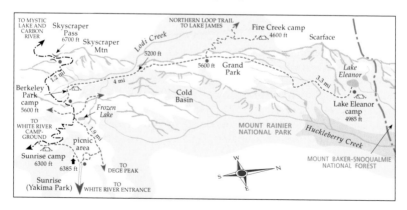

▲ *Mount Rainier from Grand Park*

and meadows of Cold Basin and climbs 300 feet to the edge of Grand Park and a junction, elevation about 5600 feet, 5.9 miles from Sunrise. The Mt. Fremont lookout can be seen above.

The Northern Loop Trail drops 2 miles to Fire Creek wilderness camp. Go right a minimum of 0.2 mile for a unique view of Mount Rainier rising above Grand Park.

For Lake Eleanor follow the almost level trail across the flower field of Grand Park another 1.5 miles before dropping into forest, at times very steeply, losing almost 800 feet. Reach the lakeshore and campsites some 10.2 miles from Sunrise, elevation 4985 feet. Having come this far, one would expect a degree of remoteness, but don't count on it. The peace and quiet are broken by a Forest Service road only 0.7 mile away.

# 31 | BURROUGHS MOUNTAIN LOOP

**Loop trip to Second Burroughs:** 5 miles
**Hiking time:** 3 hours
**High point:** 7400 feet
**Elevation gain:** 1200 feet
**Hikeable:** late July through September

If there is a trail between earth and heaven, this is it. The ridge of Burroughs Mountain, high above the White River, gives the impression of going easily onward and upward to the very tip of Columbia Crest. Any part of the walk is superb, and the first section usually is crowded with travelers aged from less than one year to more than seventy. As one goes along, the crowds dwindle. Do the walk up and back or (better) as a loop.

Note: Belying the benignity of the meadows, the trail crosses a steep snowfield that doesn't melt until August—or some years at all. Before setting out, ask the ranger about this killer snowfield—and also about its twin on the trail up from Frozen Lake, described later.

Drive from the White River Entrance to Sunrise, elevation 6385 feet. The trail starts on the south side of the parking lot and goes downhill to the walk-in Sunrise Campground.

From the campground the trail makes a stiff little climb to an overlook of the White River and Emmons Glacier—a good turnaround for short-trippers—then continues up around a slope of slabby chunks of andesite (and the snowfield that lingers late) onto a wide, flat plateau. Burroughs Mountain, like Grand Park (Hike 30), is the remnant of a lava flow that filled an ancient canyon; the displaced streams carved valleys at the sides of the flow, leaving a tableland as yet relatively undissected. In 2 miles is the 7300-foot high point of First Burroughs Mountain and the junction with the trail from Frozen Lake.

Another 0.5 mile leads to 7400-foot Second Burroughs Mountain and a memorial to Edmond S. Meany, longtime president of The Mountaineers.

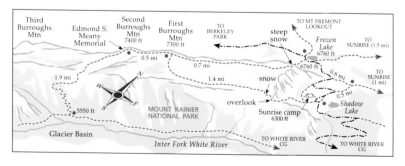

▲ *Sunrise on Mount Rainier from Burroughs Mountain trail*

No water on the high ridge, but despite that, small flowers and clumps of heather are strewn through the volcanic rubble. North is the odd, green plateau of Grand Park. West are views toward the Carbon Glacier and Moraine Park.

From Second Burroughs Mountain the trail descends 2.4 miles to the Glacier Basin trail (Hike 23), reaching it at a point 0.6 mile from the basin and 2.4 miles from the road at White River Campground.

Burroughs Mountain offers possibly the finest easily-accessible tundra in the Cascades. This plant community grows very, very slowly. The thin volcanic soil contains little nourishment, and moisture is not held long for plants to use. The growing season is short. Strong winds dry the plants and sandblast the vegetation with pumice.

In addition to struggling with these difficult environmental factors, this alpine vegetation is sometimes subjected to man's impact. Hiking off the trail causes crushing and breaking of plants, destroys seeds for future plant crops, and can reduce the small amount of organic matter in the thin topsoil. Moving rocks to make cairns or windbreaks exposes roots to drying and eventual death. Studies have shown that recovery from such stresses takes hundreds of years, even after all off-trail hiking is halted.

To complete the loop, back on First Burroughs take the Frozen Lake trail back to Sunrise (Hike 28). The distance is about the same as the other approach, and the views down into the greenery of Berkeley Park have a dreamlike quality. However, as noted earlier, a steep snow slope makes this route unsafe until mid-August or so.

# 32 | CRYSTAL LAKES

**Round trip:** 6 miles
**Hiking time:** 3 hours
**High point:** 5828 feet
**Elevation gain:** 2300 feet
**Hikeable:** mid-June through October  ⛺

**Round trip to Crystal Peak:** 7 miles
**Hiking time:** 5 hours
**High point:** 6595 feet
**Elevation gain:** 3100 feet
**Hikeable:** mid-June through October

Take your pick, a stunning view of The Mountain or crystal-clear water surrounded by alpine flower fields. Elk are sometimes seen. And frequently dogs, more of a problem here than just about anywhere else in the park.

Drive east from Enumclaw on SR 410 to the national park boundary, continue 4.5 miles, and park directly across from the State Highway Department maintenance sheds, elevation 3500 feet.

The trail begins 15 feet down the road, close to where Crystal Creek goes into a culvert. After a steady climb through forest, about 1.5 miles, a fork presents a choice between the main trail to the lake, and the unmaintained but very passable trail that leads to the lookout site on 6595-foot Crystal Peak, which has the best views.

For the lake it's onward and upward. At little more than 1.5 miles from the highway, the trail crosses the base of an avalanche slope, then makes a couple of long switchbacks upward. The third crossing gives the best look

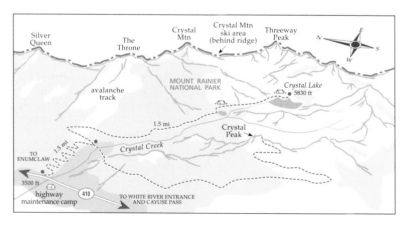

▲ *Crystal Lake*

at The Mountain, which disappears after that behind Crystal Peak (not to be confused with Crystal Mountain). In about 1 mile from the avalanche slope pass lower Crystal Lake, and in 0.5 mile more reach the 5830-foot upper and larger lake.

A number of elk and mountain goat make their summer home in this area. Look for them on slopes around the upper lake. Note the rock formations to the east; through at least two windows in the rocks can be seen blue sky.

# 33
# NACHES PEAK LOOP

**Loop trip:** 4.5 miles
**Hiking time:** 3 hours
**High point:** 6000 feet
**Elevation gain:** 700 feet
**Hikeable:** mid-July through October

An easy loop hike circling one of the guardians of Chinook Pass, passing through rich flower fields and beside two lakelets. Superb views of Rainier. Blueberries (usually) by late September. A magnificence of flaming color in autumn.

Drive east from Enumclaw on SR 410 to Chinook Pass and park, elevation 5040 feet.

The loop can be done in either direction, but going clockwise keeps Mount Rainier in front more of the time and thus is recommended. However, until late July or early August the trail along the east slopes of Naches Peak is quite snowy; unless a party is equipped for snow travel, it may prefer to set out on the counterclockwise circuit, turning back when the country becomes too white and wet for personal tastes. In such case, park at Tipsoo Lake.

To start the clockwise loop at Chinook Pass, follow the Pacific Crest Trail south over the highway on the wooden overpass. Small paths branch off left and right; stay on the main grade along the east side of Naches Peak, leaving Mount Rainier National Park and entering the William O. Douglas Wilderness.

The way traverses a steep sidehill above a green little valley, crossing several small waterfall-tumbling creeks—which, however, generally dry up in August. Flowers are at their prime roughly from late July to early

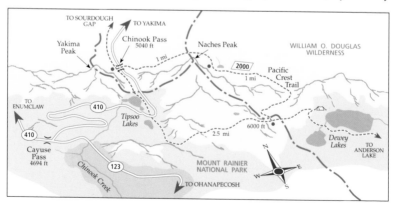

August, but some bloom earlier, some later. About 1 mile from Chinook Pass is an unnamed lakelet.

From the lakelet the trail ascends gently over a ridge, the highest point of the loop, enters the park, and at 2 miles reaches a junction. The Pacific Crest Trail goes left, dropping to Dewey Lakes (excellent camping; see Hike 34).

The loop trail goes right, over a small rise to another unnamed lakelet reflecting Mount Rainier. The way winds to high meadows on the west side of Naches Peak, Rainier always in full view, and drops back to the highway near Upper Tipsoo Lake, 0.5 mile from the starting point.

The Naches Peak loop is among the most popular hikes in the park. Even more popular, and a pleasure for anyone who can walk at all, no matter how slowly, are the two beginning and ending segments, which in a few hundred feet or any longer distance offer as nice a combination of flower-sniffing and mountain-gazing as one can find anywhere.

For a whole new experience of high meadows and The Mountain, do the loop on a moonlit night in late August or early September. Listen for the bugling of bull elk.

▲ *Beargrass and Mount Rainier from Naches Peak loop trail*

# 34 PACIFIC CREST TRAIL: DEWEY LAKES

**Round trip to Dewey Lakes:** 7 miles
**Hiking time:** 3 hours
**High point:** 5900 feet
**Elevation gain:** 450 feet in, 900 feet out

**One-way trip from Chinook Pass to Ohanapecosh**
    **Highway:** 18 miles
**Hiking time:** 2 to 3 days
**High point:** 6000 feet
**Elevation gain:** 1600 feet
**Elevation loss:** 5200 feet
**Hikeable:** mid-July through October

The Pacific Crest Trail extends from Canada to Mexico and in 1968 was acknowledged as an American classic when Congress gave it status as a National Scenic Trail. The portion of the Crest Trail running along the east boundary of the park (with frequent swings out into the William O. Douglas Wilderness) goes up and down, sometimes in subalpine forest but mostly in meadows, passing numerous lakes and ponds, waterfalls and flower fields. Occasional views of Mount Rainier and other views to peaks and valleys of the Wilderness.

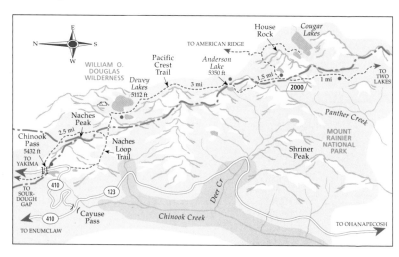

*Lower Dewey Lake from Pacific Crest National Scenic Trail* ▶

*Seed pod of the western anemone*

Whether a group is planning to hike this entire segment of the Crest Trail or only to Dewey Lakes, the best starting point is at 5432-foot Chinook Pass—rather than the 1900-foot trailhead deep in the Ohanapecosh valley. (Good access is also available at White Pass on national forest land.) To do the one-way hike recommended, transportation must be arranged.

Drive SR 410 east from Enumclaw or west from Yakima to Chinook Pass and park 0.3 mile east of the summit.

Go south on the Pacific Crest Trail, cross the highway on the wooden overpass, enter the William O. Douglas Wilderness, and in a scant 2 miles swing briefly through Mount Rainier National Park to the Naches Peak loop trail (Hike 33) junction.

Keep left, reenter the Wilderness, and descend 900 feet in a long 1.5 miles to Dewey Lakes at 5112 feet, 3.5 miles fron Chinook Pass. Good campsites at both lakes, which are outside the park. Forest Service camping permits are required. Camping is banned within 100 feet of the water. The lakes make a fine destination for beginning backpackers and small children; the round-trip distance from Chinook Pass is only 5 miles, an easy weekend.

From Dewey Lakes the trail climbs past a wide meadow-marsh laced

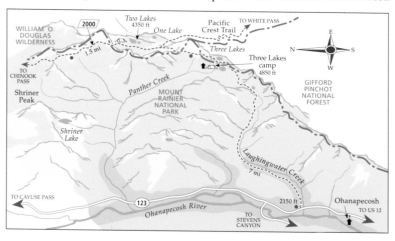

▲ *Tarn along Pacific Crest National Scenic Trail*

with meandering streams, then rounds a shoulder of Seymour Peak. At 5.5 miles is little Anderson Lake, with meadowy shores and forests on all sides. This is a good turnaround for a long day's round trip from Chinook Pass.

The trail climbs steeply a few hundred feet from Anderson Lake and reenters the park for 0.3 mile in the headwaters of Deer Creek, with views of Mount Rainier, then drops a bit, leaves the park, and at 7 miles reaches a junction with the American Ridge–Cougar Lakes trail. Keep straight. Back in the park again, switchbacks climb the forested west side of House Rock into flowers again. At 9.5 miles the way leaves the park, crosses the crest, and contours above Two Lakes. At 10 miles a sidetrail drops 300 feet to campsites at Two Lakes (no camping permit needed). The Crest Trail continues south and again slips briefly into the park and out. At 11 miles is a junction. The Pacific Crest Trail leaves the park for good and continues south 15 miles to White Pass. Keep right (straight ahead) and descend 1 mile to Three Lakes wilderness campsites (camping permit needed; Hike 37) and 6 miles more to the highway near Ohanapecosh.

# 35 EAST SIDE TRAIL

**One-way trip from Deer Creek to Ohanapecosh Campground:** 9 miles
**Hiking time:** 4 hours
**High point:** 3500 feet
**Elevation loss:** 1500 feet
**Hikeable:** June to mid-November

A forest hike near a cool river. Try it in spring when higher trails are still buried under snow or in summer when The Mountain is lost in rain or in late fall when meadowlands are a blank misery of cold-blowing storm. A wide path with little brush to moisturize clothing. If transportation can be arranged, this is an ideal one-way trip. Start at the top and walk downhill; except for the first 0.5 mile, the grade is so gentle a hiker hardly is aware of descending.

Drive the East Side Highway north 6 miles from the Stevens Canyon Entrance, or south 5 miles from Cayuse Pass, to a very small unmarked parking space 0.5 mile south of Deer Creek. Find the trailhead on the downhill side of the road, elevation, 3232 feet.

The trail drops rapidly, passing Deer Creek Falls and in a scant 0.4 mile goes to a nice campsite at the junction of Deer Creek and Chinook Creek. Here the way is joined by the East Side Trail, descending from Cayuse Pass. (For an even longer one-way hike, pick up this unsigned trail at a large parking area east of Cayuse Pass and follow it on down; to the total one-way distance add 4 miles.)

At the camp, go left. In a scant 1 mile from Deer Creek cross Chinook Creek above a pretty canyon and falls. In about 3 miles cross the Ohanapecosh over a corkscrew of a falls. At about 6.5 miles pass a sidetrail to the Grove of the Patriarchs (Hike 38). In a little over 7 miles from the Deer Creek trail cross the Stevens Canyon Road and in another 0.5 mile join the

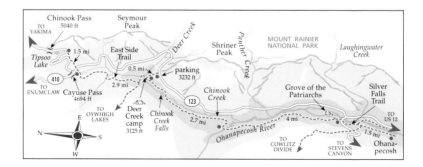

▲ *Chinook Creek Falls below East Side Trail*

Silver Falls trail (Hike 39) and hike either side of the river into Ohanape-cosh Campground.

Mostly the walk is out of sight of the river, but never out of sound. Sometimes the way is through virgin forest, occasionally crossing an avalanche slope covered with vine maple.

# 36 | SHRINER PEAK

**Round trip:** 8.4 miles
**Hiking time:** 5 hours
**High point:** 5834 feet
**Elevation gain:** 3434 feet
**Hikeable:** July through October

A lookout peak with a commanding view of the Ohanapecosh valley and Mount Rainier, and distant views of the Cascades north and south. A meadow lake in a basin below, summer home of a large herd of elk. Despite the panoramas this is one of the loneliest trails in the park.

Drive Highway 123 (East Side Highway) north 3.5 miles from the Stevens Canyon Entrance, or south 7.5 miles from Cayuse Pass, to the parking area on the west side of the road about 0.5 mile north of the Panther Creek bridge. The trail is on the east side of the road, almost hidden from sight. Parking is to the west of the trailhead, elevation 2400 feet.

On sunny days it is best to start early in the morning to beat the heat. The dusty trail swings steeply from cool forest to hot hillside, climbing through an old burn with trees too small to give much shade. In 2.5 miles the way reaches the crest of a ridge; still no shade, but the view—and possible breeze—make the rest of the hike bearable. The last 1 mile switchbacks to the 5834-foot summit and the lookout building, which is seldom staffed.

Camping is permitted near the top of Shriner Peak. Water may have to be hauled some distance. Campers definitely will want to poke their heads out of their tent at dawn to watch the sunrise on Rainier's shining glaciers.

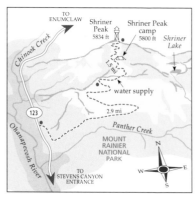

◀ *The lookout's view of Mount Rainier*

▲ *Lookout on Shriner Peak*

# 37 LAUGHINGWATER CREEK— THREE LAKES TRAIL

**Round trip to Three Lakes:** 12 miles
**Hiking time:** 6 hours
**High point:** 4678 feet
**Elevation gain:** 2550 feet
**Hikeable:** July through October

A woods trail to three small lakes and onward to the Pacific Crest Trail. Or a loitering mile through moss-covered forest to a picnic spot beside the laughing water.

Drive about 1 mile north from Ohanapecosh, or a scant mile south from the Stevens Canyon Entrance, to Laughingwater Creek. Park on the west shoulder of the highway north of the creek, elevation 2150 feet. The trail starts on the east side of the road just beyond a steep bank.

The first 1 mile, the tread smooth and grade gentle, climbs over a small knoll and drops a few inches. For those wanting a short walk this is the turnaround. But before going back, go down to the creek. Loud it is, but not "noisy"—this is the sound of wildness.

The next 2 miles the way climbs gently; water is scarce in late summer. Gradually the trail becomes steeper, crossing a small creek at about 3.5 miles.

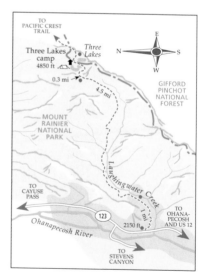

At 5.5 miles the Laughingwater Creek trail drops slightly to 4850-foot Three Lakes and wilderness campsites at 6 miles from the road. The patrol cabin, a log structure, is in a picturesque setting between the first and second lakes. Nearby is the camp area.

Follow the trail along the middle lake a few hundred feet to the park boundary and the third lake. Continue 0.5 mile, climbing from trees into open country. For views of Mount Rainier hike another 1 mile to the junction with the Pacific Crest Trail (Hike 34).

▲ *One of the Three Lakes*

# 38 GROVE OF THE PATRIARCHS

**Round trip:** 1.5 miles
**Hiking time:** 1 hour
**High point:** 2200 feet
**Elevation gain:** none
**Hikeable:** June through October **1**

The name tells the story: a virgin forest of ancient Douglas-firs, western hemlocks, and western red cedars, a place to become humble in the presence of living things that were already aged—by human measure—when the Normans conquered England. Short and easy walk along a nature trail.

Drive to the Stevens Canyon Entrance and continue 0.2 mile on the Stevens Canyon Road to a large parking lot beyond the Ohanapecosh River bridge. The trail starts behind the restrooms. Elevation, 2200 feet.

The way goes upstream through beautiful forest 0.5 mile to a junction. The nature trail turns right, to cross a suspension bridge onto an island in the Ohanapecosh River. After passing through small trees, the path forks: Go either way; it's a loop. Signs identify plants and describe features of the ecological community.

Isolated on the island and thus protected from fire, the trees have grown to gigantic proportions. In this small area are twenty western red cedars more than 25 feet in circumference; among them is the largest cedar in the park. There are ten Douglas-firs over 25 feet in circumference; one is 35 feet. The trees are estimated to be nearly 1000 years old.

*Vanilla leaf* ▶

▲ *Ancient cedar trees above a carpet of vanilla leaf in Grove of the Patriarchs*

# 39 SILVER FALLS

**Loop trip:** 3 miles
**Hiking time:** 1½ hours
**High point:** 2100 feet
**Elevation gain:** 300 feet
**Hikeable:** May through November   **1**

Tall virgin forest, a moss-carpeted floor, and a busy waterfall in the Ohanapecosh River. All on an easy loop hike up the east bank of the river, returning down the west side of the valley.

Drive into Ohanapecosh Campground and park in front of the visitor center, elevation 1950 feet.

The trail starts behind the center on the Ohanapecosh Hot Springs Nature Trail. In 0.2 mile is a junction; go right on the Silver Falls trail, passing hot springs that years ago supported a health resort. An easy grade follows within sound, if not sight, of the Ohanapecosh River, crossing Laughingwater Creek and climbing over a small bluff to a view of Silver Falls. (If the falls are one's only interest, they can be reached more quickly by taking the Laughingwater Creek trail from the highway, starting at a point 300 feet north of the Laughingwater bridge.)

At the falls the loop trail bridges a narrow rock-walled canyon, crossing from the east side of the river to the west. Look down into a deep, crystal-clear pool. The way continues upstream to a scenic overlook at the top of the falls, then a few steps more to a junction with the East Side Trail (Hike 35). Keep left to another junction within a hundred steps. Keep left again. The trail, though now headed downstream, climbs a bit before descending to the starting point.

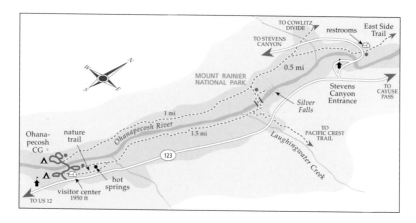

▲ *Silver Falls below trail bridge*

# 40 | COWLITZ DIVIDE

**Round trip:** 8.4 miles
**Hiking time:** 4 hours
**High point:** 4760 feet
**Elevation gain:** 2440 feet
**Hikeable:** July through September

Climb in deep-shadowed virgin forest to a junction with the Wonderland Trail. The route is often combined with the Owyhigh Lakes trail (Hike 21) and East Side Trail (Hike 35) by hikers doing the Wonderland Trail but wishing to avoid the high, snowy country of Panhandle Gap (Hike 22).

Drive from the Stevens Canyon Entrance less than a mile on the Stevens Canyon Road to a parking area and trail sign on the right, elevation 2350 feet. (The hike can also begin at Ohanapecosh Campground, though this adds 2 miles each way: From the campground follow the Silver Falls trail

▲ *Footbridge on Cowlitz Divide trail*

on the east side of the river, Hike 39; at the falls, cross the footbridge; in a few steps take a left fork and go 300 feet to another junction; take the right fork and in 0.3 mile reach the Stevens Canyon Road at the parking area.)

The first 1 mile from the parking area starts steep but soon becomes very moderate, gaining 400 feet through large trees. After a huge log bridge over a small creek the way steepens, crossing Olallie Creek (campsites nearby) in about 3 miles and in another 1 mile joining the Wonderland Trail a bit before it begins the long drop into Nickel Creek. No mountain views at this turnaround point, but the forest is reward enough.

If transportation can be arranged, a one-way trip can be made, continuing on out Nickel Creek (Hike 41).

▲ *Tiger lily*

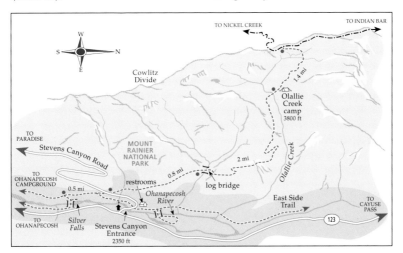

# 41 | INDIAN BAR

**Round trip:** 14.5 miles
**Allow:** 2 days
**High point:** 5914 feet
**Elevation gain:** 2900 feet in, 800 feet out
**Hikeable:** late July through September

A unique section of the Wonderland Trail. Miles of ridge-walking through alpine meadows with views of the southeast side of Mount Rainier, ending in a broad green valley into which pour a dozen waterfalls. One of the legendary places in the park. A great spot to sit in the moonlight on a late-August night and listen to the bull elk bugling.

Drive the Stevens Canyon Road west from the Stevens Canyon Entrance (10 miles), or east 11 miles from the Longmire–Paradise road, to the parking lot at Box Canyon, elevation 3050 feet. Find the signed gravel trail directly across the highway from the parking area. (Do not take the paved nature trail by mistake.) The first 1 mile is easy walking on a moderate grade to Nickel Creek. Good campsites along the stream and on the far bank. In another 0.5 mile is a small creek, the last water before Indian Bar. From Nickel Creek the way climbs steadily to the Cowlitz Divide, reaching the crest in a bit less than 3 miles from the road. Here are junctions with the trail from Ohanapecosh (Hike 40).

The next 4.3 miles are along the crest of the Cowlitz Divide, going up and over some bumps and contouring around others. At times the way is very steep. First there are glimpses of The Mountain through trees. Then the trail climbs higher, the meadows grow larger, and finally, atop a 5914-foot knoll, The Mountain comes completely and grandly into the open. To the southeast is Bald Knob. Beyond is Shriner Peak. From the knoll the trail drops 800 feet to 5120-foot Indian Bar.

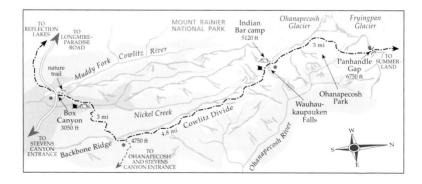

▲ *Mount Rainier and Little Tahoma from ridge above Indian Bar*

The Ohanapecosh River divides the large green meadow. The shelter cabin is on the west side of the river. At the valley head are small remnants of the Ohanapecosh Glacier. In early summer numerous waterfalls splash down the lava cliffs. Just 100 feet below the shelter is Wauhaukaupauken Falls, a name almost larger than the falls.

Don't forget the considerable elevation gain on the return hike.

If transportation can be arranged, Indian Bar can be combined with Summerland (Hike 22) for a one-way trip of 17 miles, and a beauty.

# 42 BENCH AND SNOW LAKES

**Round trip:** 2.6 miles
**Hiking time:** 1½ hours
**High point:** 4678 feet
**Elevation gain:** 400 feet in, 300 feet out
**Hikeable:** July through October

A trail with three major ups and downs, very dusty in dry weather, traversing shrubby meadows that some years have a spectacular display of beargrass and in the autumn offer the varied reds of mountain-ash and huckleberries.

Drive the Stevens Canyon Road west from the Stevens Canyon Entrance 16 miles or east 3 miles from the Longmire–Paradise road, to a parking area (elevation 4550 feet) about 1 mile east of Louise Lake. Find the trail here.

The two lakes lie at about the same elevation as the parking lot, but several low ridges must be crossed to get there. Bench Lake, at 0.8 mile, lies on the edge of a cliff amid dense thickets of slide alder. In another 0.5 mile is Snow Lake, with two of the most beautiful wilderness campsites in the park. The lake occupies a cirque below Unicorn Peak. Shaded by high ridges, snow stays late. The lake frequently doesn't melt free of snow until late July.

Around the shores are open meadows and groups of subalpine fir. Unicorn Peak, highest point of the Tatoosh Range at 6939 feet, rises directly to the south. To see Mount Rainier reflected in the lake, walk past the inlet to the far side.

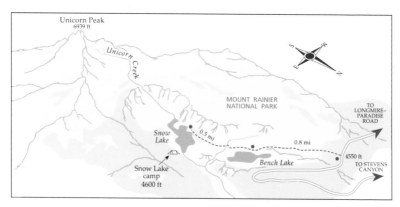

*Yellow monkeyflowers* (Mimulus tilingii) *at Snow Lake inlet* ▶

# 43 | PINNACLE SADDLE

**Round trip:** 3 miles
**Hiking time:** 2 to 3 hours
**High point:** 6000 feet
**Elevation gain:** 1150 feet
**Hikeable:** August through September

A grand view of The Mountain, from a point far enough away to see it all in a single wide-eyed look, close enough to see the fine detail of glaciers and lava cliffs.

Drive the Stevens Canyon Road west from the Stevens Canyon Entrance about 17.5 miles or east 1.5 miles from the Longmire–Paradise road, to the Reflection Lakes parking area, elevation 4860 feet. The trail starts on the uphill (south) side.

The path is gentle at first, but soon turns steep and remains so. In July several hazardous snowfields must be crossed. Use extreme caution; hikers lacking good boots would do better to give up and try again later in the season, when the snow has melted.

The view of Mount Rainier grows steadily more impressive with every inch of elevation gained; at the 6000-foot saddle is an almost equally impressive view south—across miles of forest, the village of Packwood, and the Goat Rocks—to Mt. Adams.

The trail ends at the saddle. Yet countless tourists, many in street shoes, continue to the top of 6562-foot Pinnacle Peak. Though trained climbers consider Pinnacle an easy ascent, most of the hikers who visit the summit have no business on the steep, unstable rock. They are a hazard to themselves with their slippery shoes—and a hazard to others below as they kick down loose stones.

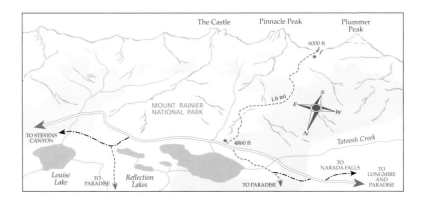

▲ *Pinnacle Saddle trail and Mount Rainier*

# 44 PARADISE FLOWER TRAILS

**Round trip:** 1 to 3 miles
**Hiking time:** 1 to 3 hours
**Elevation gain:** up to 500 feet

At Paradise the alpine fields achieve a climax unsurpassed anywhere in the Cascades. The flower season generally lasts from mid-July to mid-September, peaking the first of August. All are easily reached on paved trails. Drive to the large parking lot near the Paradise Ranger Station, elevation 5420 feet, and choose your trail for the day.

## Flower Trails  **1**

Snow doesn't leave the meadows until mid-July, but even in June flowers bloom on exposed ridges, including a large field of yellow glacier lilies on the south side of Alta Vista. A few days after the snow melts away the meadows turn white again with avalanche lilies, then blue with lupine and red with Indian paintbrush. In August the vast carpets of color yield to patches of asters, gentians, and many other flowers. In September the meadows turn a brilliant red.

Trails radiate from the Paradise Visitor Center, Paradise Inn, and Paradise Ranger Station. All are good.

## Nisqually Vista  **1**

Find the trail in the west parking lot 300 feet from the Paradise Visitor Center. The beginning is on stone steps. At an intersection in a few feet, keep left. In 0.3 mile the trail drops to a glacier viewpoint on the edge of

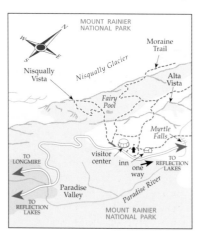

the canyon. The glacier is descending from the summit like a slow-moving river. Snow accumulates at the higher elevations faster than it melts, growing hundreds of feet deep and compressing into ice, pushing downhill at 10 or more inches a day. Some years the snout advances a few feet; other years it recedes.

## Alta Vista  **1**

For flowers and a view, the paved walk to the top of Alta Vista (the green knoll directly above Paradise Inn) is especially recommended.

▲ *Lupine in Edith Creek Basin, and Mount Rainier*

Start at either the inn or near the ranger station and follow any of the many paved trails upward through the flower fields. The wide path that makes a switchback above the inn was, in Model T days, the road to Reeces' Camp in the Clouds, located in the trees to the side of Alta Vista. Whatever route is used, avoid the extremely steep trail that climbs directly up the face of Alta Vista. Go to the left, steeply a short way, then leveling as the path contours around the backside to the top. Paradise Valley is laid out like a map with Mt. Adams and the Tatoosh Range across the way.

# 45

# SKYLINE TRAIL

**Loop trip:** 5.3 miles
**Hiking time:** 4 hours
**High point:** 7000 feet
**Elevation gain:** 1700 feet
**Hikeable:** late July to mid-October

Walk through meadows above the Nisqually Glacier to a high overlook of Paradise Valley with views of Mt. Adams, Mount St. Helens, and Mt. Hood. A good place to watch for avalanches in the Nisqually Icefall, and marmots lazing in the sun.

Drive to the large parking lot near the Paradise Ranger Station, elevation 5420 feet. The trail starts on the stone steps left of the restrooms or in front of Paradise Inn.

The first 0.5 mile, paved, climbs steeply around the west side of Alta Vista. Beyond the blacktop the way continues up the ridge toward The Mountain. Bypass the signed "Glacier Vista"; a little farther up the trail, a bit more than 1 mile from the parking lot, is an even better look over the Nisqually Glacier. A long switchback leads to 6900-foot Panorama Point, aptly named.

Views of other volcanoes to the south open up beyond the Tatoosh Range. Mount Adams, 45 miles to the southeast, has an appearance similar to Mount Rainier. The remnant of Mount St. Helens' once symmetrical cone can be seen 46 miles to the southwest; before its 1980 eruption, the volcano looked remarkably like Japan's Fujiyama. On a clear day Mt. Hood, 96 miles away in Oregon, can be seen. To the east of Mt. Adams are the Goat Rocks, the eroded roots of a once-mighty volcano.

From Panorama Point follow the trail upward another 200 feet and cross above a steep snowfield. The trail then drops gradually 1 mile to the Golden Gate trail (Hike 47), which can be used as a shorter alternate return to Paradise.

The Skyline Trail continues 0.7 mile down the ridge past the Stevens–Van Trump Memorial to a

▲ *Paradise Visitor Center (Henry M. Jackson Memorial)*

▲ *Tatoosh Range from Skyline Trail near Panorama Point*

junction. The left fork goes to the Paradise Glacier (Hike 47); in a few feet more the Lakes Trail (Hike 48) goes straight ahead. Go right, dropping into Paradise Valley. A 300-foot climb from the valley to Myrtle Falls and a 0.5-mile paved trail complete the return to Paradise.

Until early August, at least, parts of the trail are covered by snow, requiring hiking boots—unlike the paved flower walks of Paradise.

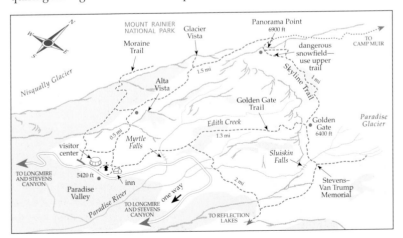

# 46 | CAMP MUIR

**Round trip:** 9 miles
**Hiking time:** 8 hours
**High point:** 10,000 feet
**Elevation gain:** 4600 feet
**Recommended:** mid-July to September

A long, arduous, and potentially hazardous ascent to the overnight cabin used by summit climbers. Climb through flowers, then rocks, then perpetual snow. At nearly 2 miles above sea level, look down on the Tatoosh Range, over the southern Cascade Mountains, and far into Oregon.

Take note: Though hundreds of casual walkers go to Camp Muir each year, this is not a trail hike. Much of the way is on snow. Part is over a permanent snowfield which is often crevassed in August and September and dangerously hard and slippery. The mountain is notorious for "making its own weather"—mostly bad. On a clear day, without warning, clouds may form, enveloping hikers in blowing fog and wiping out all landmarks. At high elevations the temperature may fall abruptly, the wind rise, and a balmy afternoon turn swiftly into a killing night. (See the discussion of hypothermia in the Introduction.)

Drive to the large parking lot near the Paradise Ranger Station, elevation 5420 feet. Follow the Skyline Trail (Hike 45) 1.5 miles. On the side of the long switchback on Panorama Point, find the Pebble Creek trail, which climbs steeply beside a small creek. The sign says, "Camp Muir 2.7 miles." But don't feel too encouraged; for the average hiker, Muir is still 4 hours away. (The 2.7 miles must be "air miles." They couldn't be "as the crow flies," since even a bird would have to circle a few times to gain all that elevation.)

The trail continues 0.5 mile to Pebble Creek, a good spot to stop for a bite to eat. From here on there

▲ *Sunrise on Mount Adams from Camp Muir*

is no trail and the route is over steep, unbroken snowfields which can be hot and exhausting.

Head upward and slightly left over the Muir Snowfield toward Gibraltar Rock. Usually the snowfield is deeply covered in snow and perfectly safe, but some years crevasses open. Be wary of small surface cracks—they mark the location of holes that underneath may be very wide and very deep. Only an experienced mountaineer can tell which line of progress is safe—and when there are crevasses, only experienced mountaineers equipped with rope and ice axes should proceed. At such time hikers would be well advised to turn around; in any event they should follow only the well-used tracks and definitely give up if the snow is soft around the cracks.

When the snow makes for difficult walking, the large rocky islands in the snowfield appear to be a seductive alternative. However, these fellfields are actually very delicate environments and should be left alone.

The view from Camp Muir is very well worth the effort. A close-up look at the Cowlitz Glacier and the rubble wall of Gibraltar. Downward, a vertical 1 mile below, the tiny buildings at Paradise. Far off, more volcanoes—Mt. Adams and Mount St. Helens, and in Oregon, Mt. Hood and Mt. Jefferson.

# 47 | PARADISE GLACIER

**Round trip:** 5.4 miles
**Hiking time:** 3 hours
**High point:** 6300 feet
**Elevation gain:** 1100 feet
**Hikeable:** late July through September

Hike through some of the finest flower fields in the park, be whistled at by marmots, then climb to views above Paradise Valley and over the top of the Tatoosh Range to Mount St. Helens and Mt. Adams. The trail ends on the barren moraines and remnants of the Paradise and Stevens Glaciers.

Drive to the large parking lot near the Paradise Ranger Station, elevation 5420 feet.

▲ *Beargrass and Pinnacle Peak from Paradise Glacier trail*

The trail starts up the stone steps across from Paradise Inn, goes right, then on a paved path rounds a corner into flower fields of Edith Creek Basin and on to Edith Creek. Take the short sidetrail to a spectacular view of Myrtle Falls and then cross Edith Creek. Beyond the bridge is a junction; keep right on the lower trail, which continues around the basin and drops 300 feet to a crossing of Paradise River. From here the trail climbs Mazama Ridge to a junction with the Lakes Trail (Hike 48). Stay left to the Stevens–Van Trump Memorial commemorating their (almost) ascent (they did not, as they claimed and was long supposed, go to the summit) of Mount Rainier in 1870. At the memorial is a junction with the Skyline Trail (Hike 45). Keep right along an old moraine. Much of this section will be across snowpatches; follow the red posts. It is essential to stay on the trail; on each side there are dangerously steep snow slopes.

The Paradise and Stevens Glaciers used to be famous for their huge ice caves hollowed out by the action of water and wind. Small caves may develop in the future, but there is so little ice left that big caves will have to wait for the next ice age.

To see more country, either of two alternate return routes may be taken. For one, turn north (right) onto the Skyline Trail (Hike 45) at the Stevens–Van Trump Memorial, go 0.7 mile and turn left at Golden Gate, descending into Edith Creek Basin and in 1.5 miles rejoining the approach trail just above Myrtle Falls; this alternate is only 0.3 mile longer than the approach but requires several hundred feet of elevation gain to Golden Gate. For another return, almost 2 miles longer, continue on the Skyline Trail to Panorama Point and then back to the starting point.

# 48 | LAKES TRAIL

**Loop trip via Reflection Lakes:** 4.7 miles
**Hiking time:** 4 hours
**High point:** 5800 feet
**Elevation gain:** 1300 feet
**Hikeable:** mid-July through September

Views, many small lakes, flowers, and forests on an up-and-down walk.

Drive to the large parking lot near the Paradise Ranger Station, elevation 5420 feet. The trail starts across the road in front of Paradise Inn or at the stone steps to the left of the restrooms.

The beginning 1.5 miles are the same as the Paradise Glacier trail (Hike 47). The first 0.5 mile to Edith Creek is paved, traversing the hill above the inn. Cross the creek on the Myrtle Falls bridge. Keep right at the junction with the Skyline–Golden Gate trail. The way traverses a bit higher, drops to a crossing of the Paradise River, and ascends switchbacks to Mazama Ridge. At a junction on the crest, turn right and leave the Paradise Glacier trail, following Mazama Ridge down from immense fields of flowers into sub-alpine forest, passing numerous lakelets to a junction. Turn right, traversing slopes 500 feet above Reflection Lakes with views of the Tatoosh Range and the lakes, and in 1.5 miles rejoin the Lakes Trail. Turn right, dropping to the Paradise River, crossing first the highway and then the river and finally climbing back to Paradise Valley. Join the Paradise–Longmire trail a short way below the parking lot.

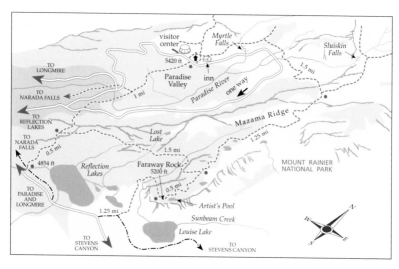

▲ *Field of avalanche lilies on Mazama Ridge*

For a slightly longer trip, with spectacular views of Mount Rainier and Reflection Lakes, at the junction continue on the Mazama Ridge trail to Faraway Rock and tiny Artist's Pool. From the brink of steep slopes beside the pool look out to the Tatoosh Range and down to the lakes. Directly below is Louise Lake. On a bench above the switchbacks on the Stevens Canyon Road is Bench Lake. To the right are Reflection and Little Reflection Lakes.

The trail descends abruptly to Little Reflection Lake and the Stevens Canyon Road. Walk along the shoulder of the road and pick up the Lakes Trail again at the first grove of trees by Reflection Lake. At the west shore is a junction. Keep right, climbing a low ridge for the return to Paradise.

# 49 PARADISE RIVER

**One-way trip from Paradise to Longmire:** 7 miles
**Hiking time:** 2½ hours
**High point:** 5420 feet
**Elevation loss:** 2700 feet
**Recommended from Paradise:** July through October
**Recommended from Narada Falls:** June through October

Start in alpine meadows, descend into forest, pass two waterfalls, and end up walking along the Nisqually River. The trip can be done in either direction, of course, but is most appealing when a party arrives at Paradise and finds the weather too poor or the snow too deep for high-country strolls. In such case don't give up the day as a lost cause: Take the downhill trail either from Paradise or Narada Falls and finish either at Cougar Rock Campground or Longmire. Obviously a member of the group must be willing to drive the car down; either that or someone must arrange a ride back to where the car was left.

Drive to the large parking lot near the Paradise Ranger Station, elevation 5420 feet. (Don't confuse this with the large nearby Henry M. Jackson Memorial Visitor Center.)

The trail begins on the south side of the lot, just where it funnels into the one-way downhill road. The trail descends to a bridge over the Paradise River, crosses the Stevens Canyon Road, and soon reaches the Narada Falls parking lot, 1.2 miles from Paradise, and then joins the Wonderland Trail.

Find the paved trail, marked "Narada Falls Viewpoint," which drops rapidly within sight, sound, and spray of the falls. The paved trail ends at the viewpoint and a fork. Continue about 500 feet to the Wonderland Trail junction. Left are the Reflection Lakes; go right, toward Longmire. In about 1 mile from Narada Falls is a bridge over the Paradise River and at about 1.5 miles, two others over small creeks. Just before the first bridge is

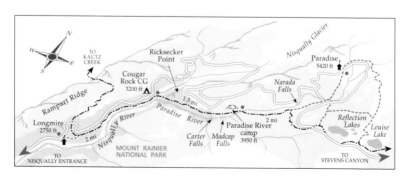

◀ *Rainbow at the foot of Narada Falls from Paradise River trail*

Paradise River wilderness camp. The altitude is now 3800 feet and large Douglas-firs appear amid the forest. At approximately 2 miles from the falls cross the wooden pipeline that used to divert water to the park's power generator. Pass Madcap Falls and watch for Carter Falls, hidden behind a curtain of small trees. The next 0.7 mile of trail more or less parallels the huge, wooden water pipes from the days when the river supplied the electricity for the park.

The valley levels off rather abruptly. South are the towering cliffs of Eagle Peak; to the north is Ricksecker Point. The trail follows the abandoned service road about 0.2 mile, crossing the Nisqually River close to the Paradise highway and the entrance to Cougar Rock Campground, 4 miles from Narada Falls.

To complete the remaining 2 miles to Longmire, don't cross the highway. Find the trail near the road and continue downhill, sometimes in sight of the river, always in pleasant moss-covered forest.

# 50 | VAN TRUMP PARK

**Round trip:** 6 miles
**Hiking time:** 4 hours
**High point:** 5800 feet
**Elevation gain:** 2200 feet
**Hikeable:** mid-July to mid-October

One of the most beautiful waterfalls in the park, flower-strewn meadows, a look at the Kautz Glacier, and a better-than-average chance to see mountain goats—for such reasons this ranks among Rainier's most popular hikes. Years and years and thousands and thousands of boots have ground parts of the trail to rough boulders and roots.

Drive 10 miles from the Nisqually Entrance toward Paradise. The trail starts at a small parking lot on the left side of the road (elevation 3600 feet), 0.3 mile before the Christine Falls bridge.

To the crossing of Van Trump Creek the way is quite steep; beyond, only fairly steep. In 0.5 mile the trail traverses the first of three avalanche slopes where snowslides annually tear out parts of the tread; the passage can be dangerous early in the season when the trail is buried under a snowfield ending in wild water of the creek; it can also be dangerous after dark, even without snow.

At 1.5 miles the track crosses Falls Creek (a fork of Van Trump Creek) and soon comes in sight of Comet Falls, 320 feet of thunder and mist. The best view is from the first two switchbacks—of the many that begin here.

Steep walking through trees and cliffs ends suddenly at the edge of the flower fields of Van Trump Park (2.5 miles) and a junction. The best view of Kautz Glacier is straight ahead on the unmaintained trail to Mildred Point, a mile farther. However, the crossing of Van Trump Creek is very

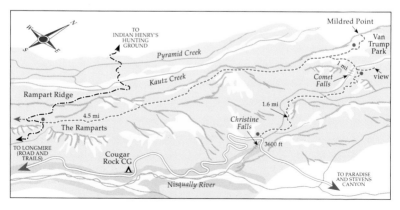

▲ *320-foot-high Comet Falls on Van Trump trail*

difficult until midsummer, so at the junction go right, climbing steeply a long 0.3 mile to a 5800-foot viewpoint.

If transportation can be arranged, a loop trip can be made by returning down the Rampart Ridge trail 4.5 miles to the Wonderland Trail junction. Take the left fork 1.5 miles down to Longmire (Hike 4).

▲ *Sunset on Mount Rainier from Road 59 on the way to Glacier View*

# OTHER TRAILS

Mount Rainier occupies some 1600 square miles. About 400 are within boundaries of Mount Rainier National Park. From park trails the hiker looks outward over the other 1200 square miles of The Mountain that are partly in national forest managed for multiple-use, partly in private ownership managed for private profit. The views inward from such trails as survive amid logging roads and clearcuts provide that one-step-back perspective that conveys the full majesty of the lofting from 2700 feet in valley forests to Columbia Crest, 14,411 feet high in the sky.

These trails are not built or maintained at the same standards as those in the park but are typically less populated. Some are in what might be considered "Park Addenda," national forest lands that were included in the Washington Wilderness Act of 1984: Clearwater and Norse Peak Wildernesses to the north, William O. Douglas Wilderness to the east, Tatoosh Wilderness to the south, and Glacier View Wilderness to the west. Other trails are unprotected.

As a suggestive sampling, following are five trails that are part of The Mountain but are not in the park.

▲ *Marmot*

# NOBLE KNOB

**Round trip:** 7 miles
**Hiking time:** 5 hours
**High point:** 6011 feet
**Elevation gain:** 500 feet in, 300 feet out
**Hikeable:** July through October
**Map:** Green Trails Lester No. 239
**Information:** White River Ranger District, phone (360) 825-6585

If you want flowers, burn the trees. As the result of a fire set by lightning (or somebody) in the 1920s, the fields of color here rival those of Paradise. In stark contrast to the at-hand yellows and blues and reds is the whiteness of the north side of Mount Rainier, not far away across the valley, close enough to see crevasses in the Emmons Glacier and cinders of the crater rim.

Drive US 410 east of Enumclaw some 31 miles to an obscure sign pointing to Corral Pass. At 55 miles an hour, one could easily miss the small sign on the right side of the highway, and the road going off to the left. Check the odometer reading at the well-signed Buck Creek forest road. In 1.3 miles from Buck Creek, pass Alta Lodge; in 0.5 mile more, turn left on Corral Pass road No. 7174. Drive 6 steep miles to Corral Pass and a junction. To the left is the Noble Knob trail, to the right, signed "Campground," is a large parking area with two trailheads, elevation 5650 feet. The Mount Rainier View Trail trailhead is on the uphill side.

The trail lies along the edge of the Norse Peak Wilderness, contouring a hillside, alternating for 0.7 mile between flowers and groves of subalpine trees, and then follows a now-abandoned jeep road another 0.8 mile. A

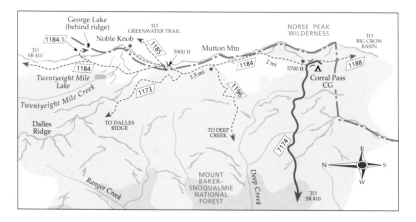

short, abrupt bit concludes with a resumption of trail. At 2 miles pass Deep Creek trail No. 1196 and at 2.5 miles reach a 5900-foot saddle. From here the trail drops steadily. At 3 miles, directly above Twentyeight Mile Lake, pass Dalles Ridge trail No. 1173. Shortly beyond, at 5600 feet, is a three-way junction.

The left fork, trail No. 1184, descends past George Lake (1 mile from the junction a sidepath contours right to the lake, 5500 feet, and campsites) to road No. 72. The right fork goes down past Lost Lake to the Greenwater trail. Take the middle trail, cross a large, treadless meadow, and with one switchback in a path overgrown in blossoms, traverse completely around the mountain to the old lookout site atop 6011-foot Noble Knob.

▲ *Lupine and Mount Rainier from Noble Knob trail*

# TATOOSH RIDGE

**Round trip to viewpoint:** 6 miles
**Hiking time:** 4 hours
**High point:** 5400 feet
**Elevation gain:** 2600 feet
**Hikeable:** July through September  ❸
**Maps:** USFS Glacier View Wilderness and Tatoosh Wilderness,
Green Trails Packwood No. 302
**Information:** Packwood Ranger Station, phone (360) 494-5515

This long ridge, with its flower meadows and beautiful lake, is, in nature's plan, an essential part of Mount Rainier. The ridge gives views not only of The Mountain but also the backside of the Tatoosh Range, whose peaks are familiar as seen from Paradise but except for Pinnacle are difficult to recognize from here. On the highest point is the site of the Tatoosh Lookout, made famous in the 1940s by Martha Hardy's bestselling book *Tatoosh*, the story of her years as a fire lookout. (The book was reprinted in the 1980s.) The wildland vista Martha Hardy celebrated was at long last (by the 1984 Washington Wilderness Act) accorded the protection of the Tatoosh Wilderness.

The trail extends the full length of the ridge, starting in the south near Packwood, climbing beside Hinkle Tinkle Creek, and ending in the north on a logging road near the park boundary. If transportation can be arranged, the entire distance can be done on one trip. It is described here from a north-end start because that way has 1000 feet less elevation gain.

From the Packwood Ranger Station at the north end of Packwood, drive west on Skate Creek road No. 52. In 0.5 mile cross the Cowlitz River. (To

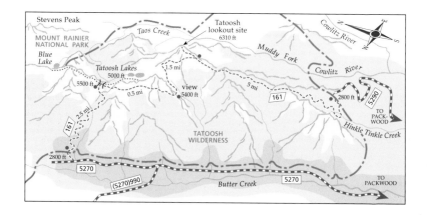

start on the south end of the ridge, cross the bridge and turn right on Cannon Road, which eventually becomes road No. 5290. Follow this upriver 9 miles to the trailhead.) For the north end continue 4 miles on Skate Creek road No. 52 from the ranger station (sign says "3"), turn north on road No. 5270, drive 5.8 miles to a junction, and there continue ahead on No. 5272 for 1.5 miles to the trailhead, elevation 2800 feet.

Trail No. 161 sets off at a steep grade, gaining about 1800 feet, climbing from Douglas-fir forest to Alaska cedar and mountain hemlock; slopes of alpine meadows begin, in season a mass of colorful blossoms. The trail makes three short switchbacks up a small stream, the only water on the main route—and in late summer, there may be none. At 2.5 miles the way comes to the crest of the ridge and a junction. The left goes to the park boundary and a possible dry campsite. Go right. Shortly beyond is a junction to Tatoosh Lakes. Proceed straight ahead but keep the junction in mind for later reference. Tread may be lost in lush greenery and soft pumice; just keep going and

▲ *Tatoosh Ridge trail and Mount Rainier*

eventually gain a ridge shoulder, 5400 feet, and a spectacular view of Mt. Adams, St. Helens, and the Cowlitz valley. To the north Mount Rainier looks down like a benevolent old lady, very fat.

After soaking up views, there are things to do, more to see. For one, continue on the trail 1.5 miles and find the mile-long spur trail climbing to the Tatoosh Lookout site at 6310 feet, highest point on the ridge outside the park, and if transportation has been arranged, descend to road No. 5290. Second, retrace steps to that first junction and follow a bootmade path to Tatoosh Lakes, a small one and a large one, on the east side of Tatoosh Ridge. From the aforementioned junction, a trail of sorts switchbacks up, crosses a 5500-foot saddle, and drops to the lakes near the outlet. But the trail can be hard to follow and cliffs make cross-country hiking tricky.

# HIGH ROCK LOOKOUT

**Round trip:** 3 miles
**Hiking time:** 2 hours
**High point:** 5658 feet
**Elevation gain:** 1400 feet
**Hikeable:** June through October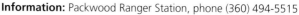
**Map:** Green Trails Randle No. 301
**Information:** Packwood Ranger Station, phone (360) 494-5515

A short but steady climb to a lookout with a breathtaking view of Mount Rainier. The cabin sits on a point of rock that juts out in the sky like the prow of a ship. A good trip for small children, but hold their hands tight on the last bit to the summit. A note of caution: Adults have been known to freeze with terror on the approach to the top and need help to get down!

Drive SR 706 toward the park's Nisqually Entrance, and a long 2 miles east of Ashford turn right on Kernahan Road, signed "Big Creek Campground—Packwood." From this junction drive about 1 mile to a steel bridge crossing the Nisqually River. At 1.5 miles is a junction. The easiest way to the trailhead is to go right on road No. 85 about 6 miles, then 5 miles more on No. 8440 to Towhead Gap, elevation 4301 feet. (This road is often damaged by slides and may not be open; check with rangers.) If road No. 85 is closed, or sidetrips to Cora, Bertha May, or Granite Lakes are contemplated, go left on road No. 52, signed "Packwood." At 4.3 miles turn

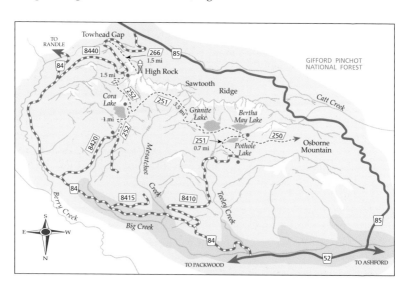

▲ *High Rock Lookout*

right on road No. 84, cross Big Creek, and start climbing. At 11.3 miles keep right on road No. 8440 and at 14 miles reach Towhead Gap.

Trail No. 266 starts on the north side of the gap, ascends a clearcut a few hundred feet, and enters forest. The first mile is mostly through trees, gradually thinning. The final 0.5 mile to the lookout is fairly open, with views to Mt. Adams and Mount St. Helens.

Climaxing all is the eye-popping panorama of Mount Rainier. Nowhere in the national park does one get this magnificent sweep from Columbia Crest down to the Nisqually Entrance. Observe the outwash from the catastrophic 1947 flood of Kautz Creek. Note hanging ice on the Kautz Glacier. Pick out peaks of the Tatoosh Range and Mt. Wow. See the green gardens of Indian Henry's Hunting Ground. When your eye shifts from The Mountain to your feet, hang on! Cora Lake is 1500 feet below, almost in spitting distance.

At midday Rainier is a big, flat curtain of white. The best views are when the sun slants over the face of the mountain, the contrast of bright light and dark shadows delineating every ridge and valley, even the trees in the parklands and crevasses on glaciers. Therefore plan to be at the lookout before 10 in the morning or after 4 in the afternoon.

To while away the midday heat and flat light, before or after the summit climb, visit lovely Cora Lake, reached by a 0.6-mile trail from road No. 8420, a spur from Big Creek road No. 84, or Bertha May and Granite Lakes, reached by a 1-mile trail from Teeley Creek road No. 8410. A very nice 3-mile trail runs along under Sawtooth Ridge, connecting the lakes, but these lakes do not have wilderness protection so there may be motorcycles.

# MOUNT BELJICA AND GOAT LAKE

**Round trip:** 8 miles including sidetrip
**Hiking time:** 5 hours
**High point:** 5478 feet
**Elevation gain:** 1300 feet in, 600 feet out
**Hikeable:** mid-July through October
**Maps:** USFS Glacier View Wilderness and Tatoosh Wilderness, Green Trails Mount Rainier West No. 269
**Information:** Packwood Ranger Station, phone (360) 494-5515

On a summer day when the hikers on trails of Mount Rainier National Park outnumber the flowers, dodge away to Glacier View Wilderness. If the meadows and lakes don't quite match those in the park, the relative solitude and unsurpassed view of The Mountain more than compensate. Beljica, an old fire watch site, is close enough to see crevasses in the mighty Tahoma Glacier but far enough away to appreciate the height as it tumbles from the summit icecap virtually to the forests.

Drive SR 706 toward the park's Nisqually Entrance and 3.8 miles past Ashford turn left on Copper Creek road No. 59. At a switchback 3.4 miles from the highway keep left at a junction, at 5 miles turn right on road No. 5920, and in 6.5 miles reach the Lake Christine trailhead, elevation 4400 feet.

For the first 200 feet, trail No. 249 ascends a steep, badly eroded ridge, then eases to traverse a very steep sidehill to Lake Christine, 1 mile, 4802

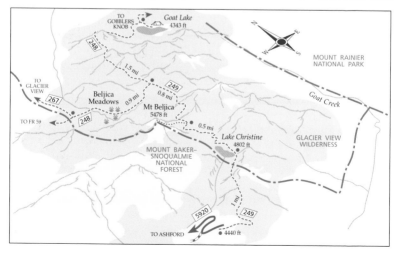

▲ *Lake Christine*

feet. Continue past the small, meadow-ringed lake and a small campsite, and climb a scant 0.5 mile to an unmarked and easy-to-miss junction. Turn left on the steep, unmaintained trail 0.5 mile to the summit of 5478-foot Mt. Beljica. Anonymous until climbed in 1897 by members of the Mesler and LaWall families, the peak's name consists of the first letters of Burgon, Elizabeth, Lucy, Jessie, Isabel, Clara, and Alex.

Fill your eyes, exhaust your camera film, return to the trail, and—if the trip is overnight—descend 600 feet more to the edge of Beljica Meadows, pass a shortcut trail to road No. 59 (see the following hike, Glacier View and Lake West), and at 3.5 miles from the car find campsites at Goat Lake, 4342 feet. The trail continues, and so can the trip, to Gobblers Knob in Mount Rainier National Park.

# GLACIER VIEW AND LAKE WEST

**Round trip:** 6 miles
**Hiking time:** 3 hours
**High point:** 5450 feet
**Elevation gain:** 1100 feet
**Hikeable:** July through October
**Maps:** USFS Glacier View Wilderness and Tatoosh Wilderness,
   Green Trails Mount Rainier West No. 269
**Information:** Packwood Ranger Station, phone (360) 494-5515

Mount Rainier—The Mountain—perhaps must be climbed to the crater, or at least explored in the zone of glacier snouts and moraines and lava cleavers, to be fully *felt*. But it is best *seen* at something of a distance, where the neck doesn't get a crick from bending back. An old fire lookout site provides a connoisseur's perspective, superior to any in the Paradise vicinity—and on a fine summer day having a hundredth or a thousandth of the human population. For added entertainment there are sidetrails to a lake and a lovely little meadow.

Drive Copper Creek road No. 59 (see the previous hike, Mount Beljica and Goat Lake) 7.6 miles from the highway to a ridge crossing with an outstanding view of Rainier. Continue on, straight ahead. At 9.1 miles is the trailhead, elevation 4400 feet.

A short trail climbs to intersect trail No. 267, built in the 1930s to help the Forest Service protect the forests from fire. Trail No. 267 parallels the road a bit, often a stone's throw from clearcuts, and enters the Glacier View Wilderness at the start of a ridge extending northward.

Hardly has the hike got started when a junction presents alternatives.

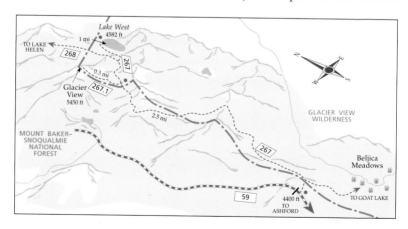

Save the right fork for the return, a 0.6-mile stroll, losing 200 feet, to Beljica Meadows, 4400 feet, a cozy marsh-meadow at the foot of Mt. Beljica (see the previous hike). This trail continues to Goat Lake and Gobblers Knob.

Go left, signed "Glacier View," along the ridge, with some small dips and lots of ups, swinging around the forested slopes of one of its summits and around the meadowy-rocky-woodsy slopes of another, to a saddle 2.5 miles from the road. Here the trail splits. The right fork drops 600 feet in a scant mile to tiny Lake West, Lake Helen a bit beyond, the pair worth an hour or two for collectors of lakes and fish.

The left fork proceeds 0.3 mile along a splinter of andesite to the 5450-foot summit, once the site of the Glacier View Lookout. You'll understand why a fire lookout was here. To the west, then, and the north and south too, the forest view commanded hundreds of square miles of ancient giants—where now are hundreds of square miles of tiny youngsters and raw clearcuts at elevations so high there'll not be a second "crop" of logs until the Second Coming.

To the east . . . the first hour you will simply gaze. Then you'll want to get out your map and methodically identify the glaciers, notably the monster ice streams of the Puyallup and Tahoma, and Sunset Ridge and Tokaloo Rock and Success Cleaver, and Klapatche Park and St. Andrews Park. By then maybe you'll be ready to visit the flowers in Beljica Meadows.

▲ *Mount Rainier from Glacier View Lookout site*

# CLIMBING MOUNT RAINIER

The summit of Mount Rainier has an irresistible attraction, and each year about 8500 people start for the summit; some 4000 succeed. There are only three regulations:

1. Climbing fees and registration are required.
2. Those under eighteen years of age must have written permission of a parent or guardian.
3. The climbing party must be made up of two or more people. (Solo climbs are allowed only with written permission of the park superintendent.)

The popular climbing season is from the second weekend in May through the second weekend in September.

Before trying for the summit, check with your physician, then get into top condition by taking strenuous hikes every weekend and jogging several miles each day. Take every opportunity to walk or run instead of riding.

There are two ways to prepare for a climb. The best is to enroll in a climbing school offered by a mountaineering club, master the fundamentals on lesser peaks, and come to Mount Rainier fully qualified to tackle it.

A second way is to join a professionally guided party at Paradise. The guide service is used by novices and good climbers short of knowledge of glacier travel and crevasse rescue. Inexperienced climbers must first spend a day at the guide-operated school learning crevasse rescue and use of ice ax and rope. Guides furnish their clients with the necessary equipment. Full information can be obtained by writing to the Superintendent, Mount Rainier National Park, Ashford, Washington 98304; or call (360) 569-2211.

Unguided parties must register and obtain a backcountry use permit at park headquarters or any ranger station. Permits are available during the hours the ranger stations are open; these hours vary.

The following personal equipment is needed: climbing boots, full-frame steel crampons (that fit), ice ax, three prusik slings, adequate inner and outer clothing, mittens, sunglasses or goggles, sun block, first aid kit, food, and sleeping bag. The following party equipment is required: climbing rope equal to or better than 7/16-inch synthetic fiber, a minimum of one 120-foot rope for each three persons, topographic map, compass, and flashlights or headlights. The following equipment is recommended: stove, matches, extra food and clothing, wands, water bottle, carabiners, hard hats, pulleys, and tarp or tent. Most of these items can be rented or purchased from the guide service at Paradise.

At the time of check-in, rangers will provide information on current route conditions. The two most popular routes to the summit are by way of Camp Muir—Ingraham Glacier and Camp Schurman—Emmons Glacier. Both require two or more days.

The first day on the Muir–Ingraham route is spent checking out and

▲ *Air view of a line of climbers on the Emmons Glacier approaching the summit crater*

hiking from Paradise to Camp Muir (Hike 46). The climb begins between 1 and 3 the following morning, to take advantage of firm snow that turns to mush under the afternoon sun. The route crosses the Cowlitz Glacier and climbs beside the Ingraham Glacier to the top, but the way changes from week to week as crevasses open and ice bridges break. Allow 6 to 8 hours from Camp Muir to the summit, and 2 to 3 hours to descend.

There is a limit on the number of people allowed to camp at each location. The limits include 110 private individuals at Camp Muir plus RMI clients, and 36 individuals at Ingraham Flats. These restrictions control numbers of climbers on a route because most climbers will need to camp somewhere. There is no specific limit on the number of climbers allowed to use a given route at any one time.

The Schurman–Emmons route is generally easier. However, the starting point is much lower and the hiking distance considerably longer. For this reason many prefer to spend 3 days on the route. From the White River Campground, follow the trail to Glacier Basin (Hike 23) and perhaps the first night's camp. Leave the trail and climb Inter Glacier to Steamboat Prow and high camp near Schurman Hut (an emergency cabin). The departure time the next morning is between midnight and 4. The route varies considerably during the summer but for much of the ascent follows The Corridor, a relatively smooth snow ridge dividing the Emmons and Winthrop Glaciers. The biggest problem usually is finding a route from the top of The Corridor through the breakups and around or over the big bergschrund near the top. Some years there isn't an easy way.

# HIKING SEASON AND TRAIL DIFFICULTY

The recommended time of year for hiking a particular trail is when the trail is generally free of snow. From year to year this varies by a week or more; for a few weeks after the recommended time, snowpatches can be expected on the trail. Above 5000 feet snowstorms occur quite frequently until mid-July and after late August and occasionally in between. However, midsummer snow usually melts in a few hours or a day.

| HIKE NUMBER | TRAIL OR SECTION OF TRAIL | MARCH–NOV | MAY | JUNE | EARLY JULY | MID-JULY | AUGUST | EASY STROLL | MODERATE HIKE | STRENUOUS HIKE | CAMPSITE |
|---|---|---|---|---|---|---|---|---|---|---|---|
| 1 | Wonderland Trail | | | | | • | | | | • | • |
| 2 | Eagle Peak Saddle | | | | • | | | | | • | |
| 3 | Longmire Woods trails | • | | | | | | • | | | |
| 4 | Rampart Ridge | | | • | | | | | • | | |
| 5 | Kautz Creek (first mile) | | • | | | | | • | | | |
| 5 | Kautz Creek | | | | | • | | | | • | |
| 6 | Indian Henry's Hunting Ground | | | | | • | | | • | | |
| 7 | Lake George | | | • | | | | • | | | • |
| 7 | Gobblers Knob | | | | • | | | | | • | • |
| 8 | Emerald Ridge | | | | • | | | | | • | • |
| 9 | Klapatche Park | | | | | • | | | • | | • |
| 10 | Sunset Park and Golden Lakes | | | | • | | | | | • | • |
| 11 | Paul Peak Trail | | • | | | | | | | • | • |
| 12 | Tolmie Peak | | | | | • | | | • | | |
| 13 | Spray Park | | | | | • | | | • | | • |
| 14 | Carbon River Trails | • | | | | | | • | | | |
| 14 | Carbon Glacier Viewpoint | | | • | | | | | • | | |
| 15 | Green Lake | | • | | | | | | • | | |
| 16 | Ipsut Creek | | • | | | | | | | • | • |
| 17 | Seattle Park | | | | | • | | | • | | • |
| 18 | Moraine Park—Mystic Lake | | | | | • | | | | • | • |
| 19 | Windy Gap—Natural Bridge | | | | | • | | | | • | • |
| 20 | Northern Loop Trail | | | | | • | | | | • | • |
| 21 | Owyhigh Lakes | | | | • | | | | • | | • |
| 22 | Summerland | | | | • | | | | • | | • |
| 23 | Glacier Basin | | | | • | | | | • | | • |

| HIKE NUMBER | TRAIL OR SECTION OF TRAIL | MARCH–NOV | MAY | JUNE | EARLY JULY | MID-JULY | AUGUST | EASY STROLL | MODERATE HIKE | STRENUOUS HIKE | CAMPSITE |
|---|---|---|---|---|---|---|---|---|---|---|---|
| 24 | Palisades Lakes | | | | | • | | | • | | • |
| 25 | Sunrise Nature Trails | | | | | • | | • | | | |
| 26 | Sourdough Trail | | | | | • | | • | | | |
| 27 | Huckleberry Creek (lower portion) | • | | | | | | • | | | • |
| 27 | Huckleberry Creek (top) | | | | | • | | | • | | • |
| 28 | Mount Fremont Lookout | | | | | • | | | • | | |
| 29 | Skyscraper Pass | | | | | • | | | • | | |
| 30 | Grand Park | | | | | • | | | | • | • |
| 31 | Burroughs Mountain | | | | | | • | | • | | |
| 32 | Crystal Lakes | | | • | | | | | • | | • |
| 33 | Naches Peak Loop | | | | | • | | | • | | |
| 34 | Pacific Crest Trail: Dewey Lakes | | | | | • | | | • | | • |
| 35 | East Side Trail | | | • | | | | | • | | • |
| 36 | Shriner Peak | | | | • | | | | | • | • |
| 37 | Laughingwater Creek Trail (first mile) | • | | | | | | | • | | |
| 37 | Laughingwater Creek Trail | | | | • | | | | | • | • |
| 38 | Grove of the Patriarchs (walk road to trailhead) | • | | | | | | • | | | |
| 39 | Silver Falls | • | | | | | | • | | | |
| 40 | Cowlitz Divide | | | | • | | | | | • | • |
| 41 | Indian Bar | | | | | • | | | | • | • |
| 42 | Bench and Snow Lakes | | | | • | | | | • | | |
| 43 | Pinnacle Saddle | | | | | | • | | • | | |
| 44 | Nisqually Vista | | | | • | | | • | | | |
| 44 | Paradise Flower Trails | | | | | • | | • | | | |
| 45 | Skyline Trail | | | | | • | | | • | | |
| 46 | Camp Muir | | | | | • | | | | • | • |
| 47 | Paradise Glacier | | | | | • | | | • | | |
| 48 | Lakes Trail | | | | | • | | | • | | |
| 49 | Longmire to Carter Falls (first mile) | • | | | | | | | • | | |
| 49 | Paradise to Longmire | | | | • | | | | • | | • |
| 50 | Van Trump Park | | | | | • | | | • | | |
| OTHER TRAILS | Noble Knob | | | | • | | | | • | | |
| | Tatoosh Ridge | | | | • | | | | | • | |
| | High Rock Lookout | | | | • | | | | • | | |
| | Mount Beljica and Goat Lake | | | | • | | | | • | | • |
| | Glacier View and Lake West | | | | • | | | | • | | • |

# INDEX

THE MOUNTAINEERS, founded in 1906, is a nonprofit outdoor activity and conservation club, whose mission is "to explore, study, preserve, and enjoy the natural beauty of the outdoors. . . ." Based in Seattle, Washington, the club is now the third-largest such organization in the United States, with 15,000 members and five branches throughout Washington State.

The Mountaineers sponsors classes and year-round outdoor activities in the Pacific Northwest, including hiking, mountain climbing, ski-touring, snowshoeing, bicycling, camping, kayaking and canoeing, nature study, sailing, and adventure travel. The club's conservation division supports environmental causes through educational activities, sponsors legislation, and presents informational programs. All club activities are led by skilled, experienced volunteers, who are dedicated to promoting safe and responsible enjoyment and preservation of the outdoors.

If you would like to participate in these organized outdoor activities or the club's classes, consider a membership in The Mountaineers. For information and an application, write or call The Mountaineers, Club Headquarters, 300 Third Avenue West, Seattle, Washington 98119; (206) 284-6310.

The Mountaineers Books, an active, nonprofit publishing program of the club, produces guidebooks, instructional texts, historical works, natural history guides, and works on environmental conservation. All books produced by The Mountaineers are aimed at fulfilling the club's mission.

Send or call for our catalog of more than 300 outdoor titles:

The Mountaineers Books
1001 SW Klickitat Way, Suite 201
Seattle, WA 98134
1-800-553-4453
e-mail: mbooks@mountaineers.org
website: www.mountaineers.org

**Other titles you may enjoy from The Mountaineers:**

**WASHINGTON'S MOUNT RAINIER NATIONAL PARK: A Centennial Celebration** *Tim McNulty & Pat O'Hara.* A large-format photographic celebration of the 100th anniversary of Mount Rainier National Park. The official book of the centennial.

**100 CLASSIC HIKES IN WASHINGTON** *Ira Spring & Harvey Manning.* A full-color guide to Washington's finest trails by the respected authors of more than thirty Washington guides.

**WASHINGTON STATE PARKS: A Complete Recreation Guide, Second Edition** *Marge & Ted Mueller.* The fully revised and updated new edition of the only guide to all of Washington's state parks, detailing facilities and four-season activities and destinations for over 200 state recreation areas.

**HIKING THE GREAT NORTHWEST: 55 Great Trails in Washington, Oregon, Idaho, Montana, Wyoming, British Columbia, Canadian Rockies, and Northern California, Second Edition** *Ira Spring, Harvey Manning, & Vicky Spring.* The latest edition of this classic hiking guide to the most spectacular trails in the region, featuring new color photos.

**BEST HIKES WITH CHILDREN IN WESTERN WASHINGTON AND THE CASCADES, Volumn Two, Second Edition** *Joan Burton.* The latest edition of one of the best-selling guides in the Best Hikes with Children series, including twenty new hikes, all ideal for families, seniors, and anyone looking for fun and easy outings.